World Flowers

Jane Packer

Photography by **Thomas Stewart**

Styling by **Lyndsay Milne**

Published in 2003 by Conran Octopus Limited

a part of the Octopus Publishing Group

2–4 Heron Quays, London E14 4JP

Visit our website at www.conran-octopus.co.uk

British Library Cataloguing-in-Publication Data. A catalogue record for this book is available from the British Library.

Publishing Director: Lorraine Dickey

Art Director: Chi Lam

Executive Editor: Zia Mattocks

Art Editor: Sam Chick

Editors: Sharon Amos and Helen Ridge

Production Manager: Angela Couchman

Styling for front and back cover and pages 1, 2, 4–5, 9, 55, 60, 61, 65, 66–7, 70, 71, 103 and 107 by Michelle Ogundehin

Flowers supplied for photography courtesy of Metz & Van Kleef, Holland.

ISBN 1 84091 326 6

Printed in China

Contents

introduction

flowers became an obsession for me at the age of 15, when I had a weekend job working in a small flower shop. At that time flowers were far from fashionable – flower arranging was most definitely a hobby for an aged aunt, and the word 'lifestyle' and all it stands for today had yet to become a part of our everyday vocabulary.

The majority of work carried out in the shop – as in so many other small family-run flower businesses at the time – tended to be low on budget and on creativity. Still, from week one I was hooked. I spent my first day's pay on a bunch of narcissi – their delicious scent was irresistible. I took them home and arranged them in a brown pottery jug with a central band of orange and yellow marbled glaze that picked up the tones of the flowers. Without even realizing it, I'd colour-coordinated container and flowers. Ever since, coordinating ingredients has become more and more exciting for me. And as an even bigger selection of flowers becomes available, my search for something new always seems to be rewarded.

I opened my first shop in London in 1982. I banned carnations and chrysanthemums with their rigid straight stems and funereal connotations, opting instead for more country-style flowers, with the idea of bringing a little nature into the city. I bought boxes of scabious, stocks, sweet William and pinks from English growers at Covent Garden Market. I asked people with gardens if I could buy their roses, lavender and hydrangeas, and at weekends I went home to my parents and cut weeds from the hedgerows – nothing was too wild for me.

INTRODUCTION

Then came a shift in flower fashion, with the rise in popularity of the fabulous, glamorous white longiflorum lilies. Long-stemmed, expensive and exquisitely ethereal, they were the media flowers of the 1980s. Of course, now lilies are available by the truckload, everywhere from florists to food stores, such is the business – and big business it is, too.

Sales of flowers have increased incredibly over recent years, with more people than ever buying flowers on a weekly basis, not as gifts but for the home. We buy them to contrast or blend with our interior styles and even to coordinate with the food we are serving – traditional, French, Italian, Japanese or Thai – you name the cuisine and there's a flower to match.

Air transport has played a vital role in making once rare and exotic flowers available worldwide. But this widespread availability is also to do with the way in which the flower industry now operates. It is no accident that as soon as lilac becomes the latest interior colour trend, several new varieties of rose become available in that same shade. Or, just as every furniture store has a brown leather sofa in the window, there is a new chocolate-coloured anthurium, gerbera or carnation on sale at the market. (And talking of carnations, they're back and acceptable again – just like flared trousers!) It's all because the flower industry is now advised by the same people who guide fashion and interior design companies on trend, texture and colour. There's a lot of money at stake for breeders or growers of the fashion flower of the moment. The industry is a multibillion-dollar business, with the Japanese and Dutch at the forefront of innovation in breeds and varieties. During my years in the horticultural industry I've visited both countries intensively and been constantly amazed by the incredible variations that are available.

In 1990 I opened a flower-arranging school in London – quickly followed by one in Japan – offering classes lasting from one day to four weeks. As I stand before a class at the start of each course I can hardly believe how international we have become. Students cross the globe to come to the school and use flowers from all over the world, working to international design trends. Influences include Bollywood, with the bright intense clashing colours of India, the Zen-like shades of green and slate from Asia, the browns and sepias of Africa. I felt it was time to record just how international flowers have become.

The aim of this book was to tell the story not only of the flowers available and a little of their history and origin, but also to introduce the various design influences of the world. I wanted to show how you can draw inspiration from interiors, furniture, food, colour and texture, and how you can blend these influences to work with flowers.

The idea is not to be tied down to what is truly natural; in any case, it is often almost impossible to know what is natural, especially when many flowers have crossed continents to be grown, then flown back and sold outside their true season. (Stocks, for example, originally from the Mediterranean, are now grown in England, Italy, Holland, Mexico and Kenya for export.) Instead, by looking closely at a flower's attributes – its personality, its texture and colour – you can combine it with other ingredients that magnify its impact.

I feel passionately about the flower business and its ever-expanding portfolio of ingredients. And now I am not alone: working with flowers is a fashionable profession with many new designers in the ranks. I take inspiration from other design fields and use their trends and directions in my work, to cope with the constant need to grow and expand horizons. Fortunately, one of the joys of working with flowers is that inspiration is never far away. On a dark grey February day in London, opening a box of fragrant tuberose that has just arrived from a climate further south immediately transports me to another place. I want to demonstrate how this is a feeling that we can all experience and enjoy.

italy

AMARETTI VIRGINIA
INGREDIENTS: SUGAR - APRICOT
KERNELS - EGG WHITE
KEEP IN DRY AND COOL PLACE

AMARETTI VIRGINIA
INGREDIENTI: ZUCCHERO - MANDORLE
DI ALBICOCCHE - ALBUME D'UOVA
CONSERVARE IN LUOGO FRESCO E ASCIUTTO

OLD ESTABLISHED HOUSE
AWARDED WITH MEDALS AND HONOURS
TRADITIONAL

VIRGINIA

KNUSPRIGE
TRADITIONSREICHES HAUS AUSGEZEICHNET MIT
MEDAILLEN UND EHRENPREISEN

dal 1860

Antica e Rinomata
Specialità

AMARETTI

ANTICA CASA CON MEDAGLIE ONORIFICENZE
PREMIATA CON MEDAGLIE ONORIFICENZE
CROCCANTI

CROQUANTS
MAISON RECOMPENSEE PAR DE NOMB
MEDAILLES ET DISTINCT

AMARETTI VIRGINIA
ZUTATEN: APRIKOSENKERNE
ZUCKER - EIWEISS
KÜHL UND TROCKEN AUFBEWAHREN

Prodotto in Italia da - Produced in Italy by
Produit en Italie par - Hergestellt in Italien von: AMARETTI VIRGINIA s.r.l.
Loc. Prapiccinin, 6 - 17046 Sassello (SA) Italy

AMARETTI VIRGINIA
INGREDIENTS: SUCRE - NOYAUX
D'ABRICOTS - BLANC D'OEUFS
CONSERVER A L'ABRI DE LA CHALEUR ET DE L'HUMIDITÉ

ITALY

IT'S ALWAYS BEEN my dream to live in Italy, to learn to cook there and to paint. There is so much I love about the country: the weather and the attitude towards life, love, food and family.

Italy has changed very little over the years that I've been visiting. People still promenade in their best clothes on warm summer evenings, with scents of cologne and fragrant flowers on the breeze. The café in the square still has its polished chrome Gaggia machine, hissing steam and making endless cups of espresso for the beautiful and the stylish seated at tables scattered across the cobbles. Delicatessens still sell their salamis, mozzarella and olives wrapped by hand in crisp sheets of waxed paper, and black-clad widows still make their way to church as the bell tolls to leave offerings of flowers at the feet of the Madonna.

I just love the nostalgia and the romance. For me Italy will be forever epitomized by Audrey Hepburn in *Roman Holiday*. The image I have of her is one of simple elegance: headscarf, sunglasses and Capri pants.

I can see this same elegance in the flowers grown and exported by the Italians. Poppies with the sheerest, most fragile pleated petals must surely have inspired the pleated silks that Italian designer Fortuny perfected in the 1920s and 30s. (The secret of the pleating process died with him and vintage dresses fetch sky-high prices at auction.) Then there are Italian ranunculus of an unmistakable *fragoli* strawberry-ice-cream pink or in shades of lemon and apricot sorbets. I've taken inspiration from these similarities as you'll see on the following pages.

Right The flowers I've used here are all grown in Italy for export around the world. To link the blooms to their native country, I chose extremely tall narrow vases to represent classic spaghetti jars. Long-stemmed flowers placed inside the vase are encased by the glass, just as the strands of pasta would be. A selection of pastel-toned flowers enhance one another. In the left-hand vase are calla lilies (Zantedeschia), which were once available only in white but now come in many colours, from softest pink ('Rosette') to the deepest purple-black 'Schwarzwalder'. I decided on 'Mango', aptly named for the colour of the fruit. The tallest vase holds gladioli, not necessarily considered the most stylish of flowers, yet used very tall en masse in the simplest of presentations, they take on an elegant new stance. Next in line are tuberoses, whose thick fleshy flowers of delicate cream brushed with a peachy pink are highly scented and long lasting. Finally, the tulips, which are distinguished by stems three times the length of the average tulip – they are available in white, yellow, pink, orange and red. There is no easy way to position the flowers in these vases – you just have to drop them gently into place. You'll need to use a watering can to fill the taller vases, which, I have to say, are a devil to clean – attaching a brush to a long stick is the best way – but they are well worth the effort.

Previous pages The exquisite translucence of poppy and ranunculus petals is mirrored by the creases on the crumpled wax amaretti wrapper. I find the similarities between petals and paper absolutely fascinating.

PETAL ROSARY *(right)*

Although I'm not a Catholic, I know that the rosary plays an important role in the lives of many Italians. The word rosary originally meant garland, and it seemed appropriate for me to re-create the beauty of a rosary with a garland of stocks and tuberose strung on florist's reel wire.

1 Cut a length of wire at an angle so that it is as sharp as a needle.

2 Cut the flower heads of the stocks, leaving just a little stem.

3 String the flower heads as you would beads onto a needle and thread, piercing the wire through the centre of the flowers, from the base to the top. Hold the wire close to the tip, just as you would hold a needle.

4 Once the garland is long enough, knot the two ends of the wire together. Add one or two tuberose heads to each end of the wire to act as end beads by piercing the base of the tubular flowers with the wire and wrapping it around the flowers to fasten.

Above This is the perfect parade for the centre of the dinner table – witty and sophisticated without being obtrusive. Opaque Italian white glassware has been filled with red-tinted water, to make it look as rich and as red as a good Chianti. You can buy florist's colourings that not only change the colour of the water but also help to keep the water clear. Experiment with the number of drops you add until you get the colour you want.

I've placed white arum lilies in the glasses, but I can see the effect working equally well with other white lilies. In either case, cut the flower stems to length so that the petal cone sits gently on the edge of the vase, leaning gracefully to one side. This is a one-off arrangement – after an evening in coloured water the flowers may start to take on a red tinge.

NEVER ON A SUNDAE

Flower heads as rounded as scoops of soft ice cream and in ice-cream colours – the connection was just too good to ignore. For this display I've assembled deliciously delicate ranunculus in the perfect imitation of an ice-cream sundae. As well as a sundae glass, you'll need coloured gravel and a block of florist's foam.

1 Fill the bottom of a sundae glass with coloured gravel.

2 Place a small, roughly dome-topped cube of pre-soaked florist's foam on top of the gravel, and trickle more gravel around the sides of the foam to hide it completely from view.

3 Cut the ranunculus stems to about 5cm (2in) in length.

4 Start adding the flowers at the base, pushing 2.5cm (1in) of stem into the foam, and work your way upwards. The vaguely dome-shaped block of florist's foam helps create the gently rounded effect.

That great 1950s classic, the ice-cream parlour, with its Formica-topped tables and tall sundae glasses brimming over with the best ice cream ever, is a regular sight in Italy. This display would be perfect for a child's or teenager's birthday, or even a bridal shower.

INDOOR OLIVE GROVE *(left)*

The fruit of the olive tree has been pressed to make oil for centuries, and it is so intrinsically woven into the Italian way of life that it's impossible to imagine Italy without the tree or the fruit. Gnarled olive trees are to be seen everywhere in the sun-drenched Mediterranean, yet elsewhere they are still something of a novelty. Suddenly the olive is *the* shrub to have.

The smaller versions of olive trees are inexpensive and look great both inside the house and out. Here I've used tall rectangular glass vases with a deep layer of white sand to complement the silvery olive leaves. Repeating an image in this way makes a display graphically strong and impressive.

1 Half-fill three tall rectangular glass vases with white sand.

2 Hold each plant by the stem and knock the pot away from the roots with a downward blow. Brush the excess compost from each root ball to emphasize their circular nature.

3 Lower each plant onto the sand. This is a temporary display as it is difficult to water the plants without discolouring the sand. Olive trees do not require daily watering, so you could leave the display for up to a week.

Above I love the roadside shrines you come across in Italy, often in the most remote spots yet still cared for devotedly. Candles, single blooms, photographs and sacred hearts sit within the shrine on the whitest embroidery or lace. I've taken the idea of combining random containers, candles and individual flowers and bought it into the home, creating a pleasing yet inexpensive display that takes no time to make. Just choose the flowers – I've used perfumed jasmine, scented geranium and carnations – cut the stems short and arrange them in an assortment of glass containers so that they just overhang the lip.

Poppies and Pastels

Italian poppies are a favourite of mine. They arrive at the flower market still in tight bud, completely enclosed in cellophane bags bearing an Italian label. Then the petals begin to emerge from their animal-like hairy casing on long tubular hairy stems. I almost laugh out loud each time I look at them in full flower, with their petals like wonderful pleated silk ball gowns in glorious colours, yet beneath this extravagance an ugly stem. They remind me of a woman caught on camera in a beautiful dress with her hairy legs exposed – oh, the horror and embarrassment!

The poppies are available in colours that range from the sharpest orange and yellow to the palest apricots, creams and pinks. To exaggerate their colours in this design I've mixed them with pastel pink and orange genista, another Italian-grown flower export. Genista has a sweet fragrance, almost like bubblegum, and delicate hair-like stems that support ethereal flowers. The stems bend and arch naturally, making them perfect for vase displays where they will tumble gently over the rim.

1 Start by resting strands of genista and poppies over the rim of the vase. Use the normal bend in the stems to your advantage, but let them curve outwards and not towards the centre. While there is no specific ratio of genista to poppies, I would suggest ten strands of genista to five poppies.

2 Gradually build up your design from the edges towards the centre of the vase until eventually you are positioning the stems almost upright. Keep the stems all the same length and use the angle they are positioned at to create the gently curving dome shape to echo the globe-shaped vase.

caribbean

O VER THE YEARS, I've been extremely fortunate to have visited a number of Caribbean islands, and the impression I have of them is one of overwhelming warmth. The warmth of the climate is obvious – it hits you like a wall as you step from the plane. But it's also the warmth of the people: laughing children on their way to school, women shrieking in the market at a joke, men in bars enjoying rum and watching the world go by, all to the constant background beat of reggae. The colours of the Caribbean are overwhelming, too – the turquoise sea, the shades of pink, green and peach of the small fishing boats. In the market you'll see displays of fish in glistening silver and fruit-punch colour combinations of red, russet and pink, and water melons with their green dappled skins piled high, one or two ripped open to reveal glorious mouth-watering coral flesh that echoes the colour of ginger lilies and anthuriums.

Until recently I almost disliked anthuriums – I think it had a lot to do with the unreal thick and fleshy texture of the flowers. For a long time the varieties available were very limited: a peachy colour and a vivid London-bus red were all you were likely to find. Then somebody, somewhere, realized its value, that its incredibly long life span could actually be capitalized on if only it came in other colours – and now it does. We have the most amazing green varieties, 'Midori' and 'Pistache', 'Terra' is the shade of terracotta earthernware, and 'Choco' the colour of melted chocolate.

Ginger lilies (*Heliconia*) share the same rigidity of stem as anthuriums and also have a long life span, which is invaluable in warm environments or where the flowers are left untended for long periods. Contract florists know all about this, thanking their god on a daily basis for a flower that remains unflagging for more than two weeks.

Used in the right way, exotic Caribbean flowers take on a contemporary air. Arrange them simply in single colour blocks in bold vases and they reinvent themselves. En masse, they are a garish riot of uncontrolled colour – not everyone's cup of tea I know, and I have to admit, it's not mine.

Flowers from the Caribbean are imported all over the world throughout the year, bringing with them sunshine, warmth and bright colours – not to mention a touch of the exotic – even on the dullest winter day.

Left *Like shells in a transparent sea, peach anthurium flowers are encased in cylindrical vases of turquoise water. The flowers have been lined up beneath one another and held in place with small sections of florist's wire twisted around the stems. Cutting the base of the stems level helps them to stand upright in the vase. The water has been tinted with florist's colouring and the flowers kept above the water line. When displaying more than one vase, keep the water levels and the position of the flower heads consistent.*
Previous pages *A highly glossy conch shell juxtaposed with the artificial fake-plastic texture of an anthurium flower and a real plastic ball.*

CARIBBEAN

Right When choosing flowers and their containers, I love to pick up on details in the surroundings intended for the display; when these all work together well, the effect of the display is so much more dramatic. Here the combined elements complement one another perfectly: the brickwork pattern of the floor, the oblong cuts in the Perspex (Plexiglas) vases and the square brick-like fingers of baby bananas forming on the stems. Your local florist may not stock banana stems, so you may need to order them in advance. They will be expensive but, on the other hand, they will last a long time – a month, perhaps even longer, in water – so you do get your money's worth. Just make sure that you change the water regularly.

Splotched with cream and pale green where the pigments

interact, these philodendron leaves are as vast as a crow's wings

and twice as beautiful. In plain glass vases set against a white

wall, their effect is cooling and calm, simple yet dramatic.

Left *These huge variegated philodendron, or elephant's ear, leaves are simply stunning. The stems of three of the leaves have been cut off to make them flexible enough to curl around the insides of the tall glass vases before pouring in the water – a neat way of adding interest to a plain container. The stems of the three remaining leaves have been left long so that they reach the bottom of the vase, and angled so that each leaf leans slightly to one side. Keeping the water level to a minimum will help the arrangement last longer by ensuring that the curled leaves are only partly underwater.*

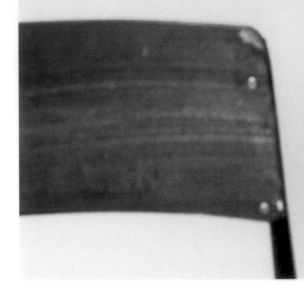

DRIFTWOOD AND SAND

The colours and textures of the components in this table centrepiece suit its basic beach-hut-style surroundings. To make this design you will need branches of sugar cane, a small amount of sand, a shallow Perspex (Plexiglas) tray, two florist's water vials and two 'Safari' anthurium flowers.

1 First fill the tray with sand. Cut the sugar cane into lengths slightly longer than the width of the tray. Then position pieces of cane across and around the tray, rather like building a raft. Use a glue-gun to keep the canes in place or bind them in position with short pieces of florist's wire.

2 Cut the anthurium flowers to length and push the cut ends into the water vials to keep the flowers fresh. Submerge the water vials in the sand but leave the rims showing to make it easier to top up the water – you'll need to do this about once a week for anthurium flowers; less robust flowers such as roses will need topping up every day

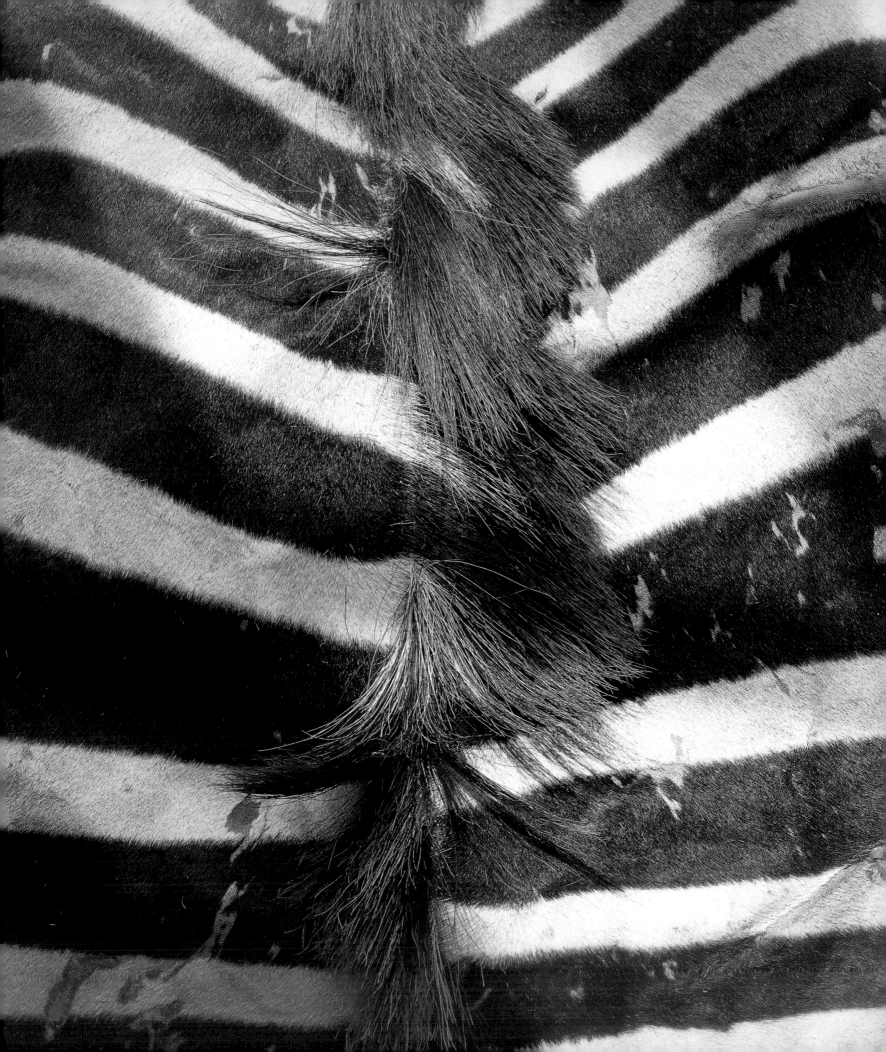

south africa

t

HE COLOURS of South Africa are what first come to mind when I look to the country for inspiration for my flower designs. I picture the sun-baked earth, in tones of russet, red and ochre, and the woven fabrics of the traditional dress. I also imagine the sun and heat and dry, dry air and the need to escape to the coolness and calm of homes with their stone floors and whitewashed walls. The garden route running along the Cape coast and the wonderful beaches also play a part in my inspiration; so, too, does the country's history of mining precious stones and metals.

The flowers of South Africa are strong and earthy, almost animal-like, and they reflect the sturdiness and resilience of the nation. I love the textures of South Africa's national flower, the protea, with its cone-shaped flower head – there is such an incredible rawness about it. Of the many varieties available, the biggest is the king protea, which is a soft metallic pink with a pale creamy centre. Others have flowers in shades of red and orange. All of them last well in or out of water, eventually drying to a range of camouflage tones: clay, earth, wood and stone.

I feel that the extraordinary flowers of the bat plant evoke the mystery and ancient history of South Africa, and I've used them to highlight the traditional figures and masks carved from blackened and polished wood. The bat plant (*Tacca chantrieri*) is absolutely incredible. It has an eerie, even sinister, appearance, and the flowers have a leathery texture, reminiscent of tribal war trophies. Strangest of all, the flowers are shiny black with thread-like tendrils that hang from the withered centre. This, in turn, is suspended on a thick foliage-free stem. At the base of the tall stem, glossy black-tinged foliage reaches skywards.

Whenever I think of South Africa, I immediately picture the parched sun-baked earth stretching out for miles all around. The otherworldly protea, in particular, evokes this harsh, almost primeval landscape for me.

Right *The bat plant is currently not imported as a cut flower, so the blooms featured here have been cut from the more readily available houseplant. Their stems have been pushed into florist's vials hidden by a pile of fool's gold, or iron pyrites. These luminous metallic rocks form a miniature landscape that supports the striking flower heads. The impression created is earthy, a celebration of the many mineral and floral aspects of South Africa.*

Previous pages *A zebra hide mirrored by the colour and texture of white sand, petrified wood and a stem of* Heliconia 'Shakos' *– the plant's downy covering giving it the appearance of animal fur. Although not South African in origin, this heliconia shares many of the characteristics of native plants, which were developed to enable them to flourish in a hostile environment.*

Left *Osteospermums, or Cape daisies as they are more commonly known, are native South African flowers and an obvious choice for this rather quirky display of painted ostrich eggs and white sand. The Cape daisy is usually available as a nursery plant rather than as a cut flower, and for this table decoration blooms have been cut from the plant and placed in water in a florist's vial hidden inside each egg. The eggs have been blown then sprayed with black paint; I chose black to highlight the centre of the flower and the tabletop. An unconventional choice of container, ostrich eggs are surprisingly robust. The landscape of white sand spread along the table is functional as well as symbolic – it stops the eggs from falling over.*

Left Proteas are very much a product of their environment, with their thick and unyielding stems that are able to withstand the strongest gusts of wind – and challenge the florist's scissors. Their oval to triangular leaves are thick and fleshy so that they can retain as much water as possible. Even the petals are sturdy: fibrous and woolly, almost felt-like in texture. Proteas endure and survive intense burning heat and dry sun-baked landscapes – delicate is not a word that I'd ever use to describe them.

I've always believed that one flower can make as much of a statement as a hundred; it all depends on the flower and what you do with it. A king protea wrapped in a swathe of pink suede exemplifies this. The protea is a statement flower – large, dramatic, intriguing in form and texture – with nothing subtle about it at all. I've often thought it has a prehistoric, almost animal-like feel, so I've exaggerated this by presenting the protea in a texture that matches the flower. Tied with a thick cord of woven rattan, the look is both organic and modern, and one that is suitable as a gift for a woman – or man – who appreciates attention to detail.

Right Pincushion proteas in a wooden bowl of dusty pink sand re-create the colours of the sunbaked landscape. I wrapped a block of pre-soaked florist's foam in plastic to stop the water from seeping out, then surrounded it with coloured sand. The proteas have been cut short and pushed into the foam at varying angles; some of the flowers are more fully open than others. I love the unbelievably artificial-looking 'nylon' threads that form their flower heads. In the trade we call the woody stems, which I've used at an oblique angle in the display, 'lipsticks'. Grown in Costa Rica, there are two species available: those with bands of brown and pink on the stem, as I've used here (Costus stenophylus), and those with a bright red flower cone at the very tip of the stem (Costus spicatis), which looks very lipstick-like indeed. These plants come from the same family as ginger lilies.

Left *I love to play with ways in which flowers are displayed; too often we restrict our imaginations by always resorting to vases. Here intricately woven tribal baskets are filled with bunches of protea. You can either stand the flowers in the basket and leave them to dry naturally, when their colours will gently fade over time, or place them in a concealed container of water – the effect is almost living art. I love the dusty hues and the texture of the petals against the bitter-chocolate colour of the wall behind. The atmosphere created is one of fading light on a baking hot evening.*

In South Africa the colours of the landscape suffuse daily life:

the houses with a textured baked-earth finish, natural ochre and

umber-dyed fabrics, the sandy browns of the soil as it is being

worked – it's like looking at the world through a sepia wash.

england

NGLAND, A NATION of gardeners. The English are famous for talking about their gardens – or the weather. Not everyone does, of course, but as a national stereotype it's still pretty accurate.

When I opened my first shop in London's West End, my aim was to introduce a little of the English countryside to town. I banished rigid-stemmed carnations and chrysanthemums, and opted instead for garden roses, wild flowers, weeds from the hedgerows and sunflowers. At the time, sunflowers were grown by farmers for their oil, not as cut flowers by commercial nurseries – that wasn't to happen for almost another decade.

The traditional cottage garden, filled with such flowers as stocks, peonies, larkspur and delphiniums, is thought of as quintessentially English, but it turns out that few of the flowers we assume to be English are, in fact, native plants – many were introduced by the great plant hunters of the nineteenth century. In spite of the cottage garden tradition, looking to the past doesn't really give a true picture of English life. Minimalism, modern architecture and furniture design play an important role in the ground-breaking country we know today, and these areas have, in turn, had an enormous effect not only on the flowers we choose to have in our homes but also on the ways in which we use them.

Even so, I believe that there is still nothing quite so typically English as taking tea on the lawn in an idyllic garden, surrounded by flowers, butterflies and bees. I've used such a setting as the inspiration for the displays in this section, creating the look with flowers that have a nostalgic, vintage appeal. Feminine, dreamy, faded antique shades of lilac, pink, green and blue, put together in simple uncomplicated ways, sit easily in homes as well as cafés and restaurants, but they are also dramatic enough to be used for marking important events.

Left *I've called this design 'Wallflower' because it reminds me of a 1950s village hall with girls in floral dresses sitting patiently, waiting to be asked to dance. On the left lilac stocks stand in a container of water inside a vintage enamel flour bin. The flowers have a wonderful fragrance similar to the scent of cloves and are delicately crumpled; the veined texture of the petals is the norm, not a sign of inferior quality. The thing to look for in stocks is good strong foliage: it should be thick and fleshy with a silvery fur-like texture. Don't buy limp, light green stems – they won't last. It's essential to change the water daily as the stems of stocks deteriorate rapidly, turning the water cloudy. The pink plastic woven basket on the right holds sweet peas, white peonies and lilacs, producing an intoxicating mix of scents. The flowers have been pushed into a block of florist's foam and the basket has been lined with plastic to prevent any water seeping through.*

Previous page, left *A pretty polka-dot shoe tidy plays an unusual role, filled with peonies, lilies, hydrangeas and roses, each in a florist's vial of water. Peonies are now sold as cut flowers, both the multi-petalled (lower centre right) and the flamboyant single types (lower centre left). The petals of single peonies tends to unfurl to reveal clashing stamens.*

Previous page, right *Available in all sorts of glorious colour combinations, pansies have a child-like charm about them. The flower heads are resting on the rim of an old china cup set on a 1950s plastic lace tablecloth. I remember my great-grandmother had a tablecloth just like this one for everyday use – the real thing was kept for best. Although utilitarian and wipe-clean, the cloth still manages to give the illusion of being made of lace.*

Left Using old and antique glass bottles along this windowsill to hold individual stems means a little goes a long way. It also allows the beauty and detail of each stem to be seen and admired rather than be lost among a mass of blooms. The hues and tones of green and pink hellebores, purple and black fritillaries and purple thistles all link with one another, as well as echoing the colours of the sofa. A display using a more random selection of flowers without any colour coordination would not be as effective.

Below Hydrangeas in delicate shades of peach and cream, parrot tulips, a peony with bold yellow stamens and a tall feathery astilbe are brought together as a display, even though the containers are all very different. Placing individual flowers in small vases instead of grouping them together in one larger one takes up more space – another example of how a few flowers can make a big impact. The key to success is choosing interesting containers that complement the colours and combinations of flowers.

Out to Grass

Some gardeners are obsessed by lawns, and here I've used the idea of a lawn as a humorous table centrepiece. I always try to make some kind of personal connection in my work, if possible – you can imagine this display at a cricket club lunch or perhaps at a dinner for horse trainers or even a convention of lawn-mower manufacturers! To create this display, you will need a series of fairly deep, rectangular Perspex (Plexiglas) trays, potting compost, individual sagina plants (a type of pearlwort commonly known as Irish or Scotch moss), marguerite daisies and florist's vials.

1 Fill the trays with potting compost. Plant the sagina plants neatly and evenly in the trays to convey the impression of a typical lawn. If you can't buy sagina, camomile or helxine plants would be fine, or even pieces of actual turf or pots of wheat grass replanted into the trays.

2 Cut down the stems of the marguerite daisies and put the individual flower heads into the florist's vials. Push these down into the compost. Marguerites are sold both as cut flowers and as pot plants – either will do here, as you need only the flower heads. Line the trays up just as they have been down the length of this boardroom table.

3 Expand on the theme and use the 'lawn' as the base for a display. Stand something taller in the centre of the grass: a stone garden urn filled with flowers or perhaps a steel watering can holding blooms – the perfect arrangement for a summer garden party or wedding.

Above *Nostalgia for my school days prompted me to come up with the idea of a nature table. At my primary school every classroom had one; it normally displayed a rather dubious collection of things, and the girls were often heard screaming as the boys performed their latest annoying prank with a worm or a piece of seaweed. There were beans growing on blotting paper, an old fish tank filled with leaves and debris that was home to silvery, slippery slow-worms, and a fossil or two. The odd glass jar with a pierced paper lid contained a caterpillar or chrysalis, and another filled with water was home to tadpoles. There was also, of course, a collection of foliage, fruit and flowers – perhaps the first acorn of the season, a stem of wild buddleia or a huge gloriously scented rose from the teacher's garden.*

For my interpretation of the nature table, I covered my kitchen table with a selection of vases and jugs, all of them from different eras but all in soft shades of blue. In them I've placed individual stems of summer flowers – sweet peas, peonies, alliums and hydrangeas, as well as commercially grown bluebells and lilac, in an attempt to excite my own children's interest.

Right *This display makes a pretty, nostalgia-filled alternative to a table centrepiece – it's reminiscent of afternoon tea at a maiden aunt's, with the cakes the only part of the visit to look forward to. I've stacked four traditional glass cake stands on top of each other with each tier displaying paper cases of flowers instead of cakes. The paper cases are watertight, so the flower heads can be placed directly in them. When preparing the arrangement in advance, wrap a piece of moist cotton wool around the base of each flower stem or push the stem into a small amount of wet florist's foam to stop the flowers from wilting. The appearance of frosted icing is created by 'Dolce Vita' roses, the white hydrangeas are convincingly meringue-like and the bright pink 'Jacaranda' roses look good enough to eat. The overall effect is a glorious confection of colour – but without a single calorie in sight.*

ENGLAND

This page Old tea caddies hold a collection of blue flowers. There's a real mix of the seasons here: autumnal deep blue hydrangeas, spring grape hyacinths, high-summer cornflowers and late summer hydrangeas of the palest cloud-like blue. The simple straightforward way in which the flowers have been used gives the impression that they have just been picked from the garden. But any gardener will know that this would be impossible. To achieve such an unseasonable combination, with spring and summer blooms side by side, I have used flowers that have all been imported. By stretching a species' season to make its flowers available all year round, we can re-create the joy of spring or summer in the middle of winter.

Colour is a strong influence in any display and one that can go a long way to suggesting a season, too. Reds and rust immediately say late summer leading into autumn, while white, soft pinks and lilacs have a hazy hint of high summer about them. In this display shades of blue against a cool white background have a definite spring-time air.

france

Y

EARS AGO I remember visiting Paris and gazing through the windows of a smart city florist, its decor all veined marble. The vases were of sparklingly clear glass and the soaring stems of delphiniums. roses, lilies and peonies, all unbelievably long – I'd never seen flowers so tall and of such exquisite quality. The shop was elite and expensive, the staff aloof and snooty – a sign saying *'Vous êtes priés de ne pas prendre des photos'* summed up the atmosphere. My lasting impression was one of exclusivity; the shop had much in common with fashion and *haute couture*.

At that time at the Paris flower market I found wonderful elongated antirrhinums, peonies and lilies – I've never seen them quite like that anywhere else. There were roses that you just had to bury your nose in, heavenly scented, all home produced and taken to market by small family growers. Sadly much of this tradition has disappeared; the large commercial importers have taken over, but I still feel there are flowers that say France.

In my designs I've used the idea of Parisian chic to pay homage to a country that epitomizes style. The fashion houses – Dior, Chanel, St Laurent, Givenchy – are an obvious source of inspiration. Christian Dior's signature flower was lily of the valley, a keynote in fragrances such as Miss Dior and Diorissimo; Coco Chanel used the camellia as her signature flower in the 1920s and 30s, in everything from jewellery designs to fabric corsages; and Karl Lagerfeld has revived the camellia corsage in recent Chanel collections.

Right *As a child I remember being fascinated by the precious bottles of perfume my mother kept on her dressing table. There was a sense of glamour about them but also a hint of something forbidden. The intrigue continued when I first saw the huge display bottles in department stores, with their air of extravagance and wantonness. I wanted to evoke this idea of a glamorous bedroom, un boudoir risqué, by using scent bottles filled with flowers set against a very 1930s decor. Roses have a timeless quality, an almost vintage feel that suits the room perfectly. I sprayed large white roses with gold florist's paint to heighten their air of opulence. The paint dries in minutes and doesn't damage the flowers, which last as long as normal or sometimes even longer as the paint hides any signs of ageing or browning. There is something about this technique – that of adorning a beautiful flower to make it even more beautiful – that is symbolic of a woman applying her make-up, or dabbing her wrists and neck with perfume.*

Previous pages *The Chanel button is a style icon – so, too, is the gardenia. This luxurious milky white flower is prized for its exquisite fragrance. Fleshy in texture, the petals bruise easily, making them difficult to import en masse.*

AUTUNNO INVERNO 1992-93   N. 23

=GARBO=
A Portrait by Alexander Walker
AUTHORIZED BY METRO-GOLDWYN-MAYER

WEIDENFELD
& NICOLSON

ABRAMS

Left Three identical shallow glass bowls hold short stems of gardenia flower heads, still with their leaves attached. The water level in each bowl is roughly the same and there is just enough water to cover the end of the stems. I've used up to three flowers in each bowl and cut the stems at an angle to maximize the uptake of water. Stacking the bowls one on top of the other creates visually interesting translucent layers of glass and water.

Above The combination of crystal-clear glass and pure white flowers will always lend an air of sophistication to an interior. Here I've displayed the gardenia layers alongside elegant trails of fragrant stephanotis, spheres of white roses piled within a glass tank and tied bunches of lily of the valley, making the perfect adornment for a glass and chrome side table. Turn the page to see how to make the spheres of roses.

A SPHERE OF ROSES *(right)*

Spheres of flowers look fabulous, yet are quite simple to make. Stacked in a glass vase (see previous page), they're real show stoppers. You can also use this technique to make a topiary tree by impaling the sphere on the tree 'stem'. For a pomander, attach a ribbon to a length of florist's wire and push it through the centre of the sphere before adding the flowers.

1 Cut a sphere from a block of florist's foam by gradually slicing away until you have a reasonably round shape – it needn't be perfect as you won't be able to see it. Leave it to soak in water, then lift it out to drain for two hours so that it won't drip.

2 Cut the rose stems, at an angle, so that they are about 2.5cm (1in) long. As well as improving the uptake of water, this also makes it easier to push the stems into the florist's foam. Remove any foliage.

3 Make a row of flowers around the sphere, pushing them firmly into the florist's foam so that they touch each other.

4 Make another row of flowers at right angles to the first, dividing the sphere into quarters. Then fill these quarters in with flowers.

Left Lily of the valley is available during its natural season in spring – and throughout the year, but at a price. Different in form from its garden relation, this is the aristocratic version: taller and paler stemmed, with less robust, almost papery foliage. Growers force the plants into flowering by giving them an artificial winter and early spring. In the market they're sold with roots attached to extend their fragile life. More often than not, lily of the valley is destined to be an element of a bridal bouquet, but for anyone with the means to afford it, it can make an incredibly beautiful and indulgent gift.

SHEER GLAMOUR *(opposite)*

Christian Dior is quoted as saying: 'I created flower women with gentle shoulders and generous bosoms, with tiny waists like stems and skirts belling out like petals.' I've reversed the analogy here by turning flowers into a fashion accessory – an evening bag made of gold.

This design can be made in different shapes and sizes, and with very different flowers. It's a fantastic idea for a girl's birthday party, baptism or, as I have done here, as a gift for a VIP fashion journalist, posed on a front-row catwalk seat. In this instance, I've used white roses sprayed with gold florist's paint to imitate the texture of the soft gold leather of vintage dancing shoes and matching purse. The other materials you will need are a block of florist's foam, chicken wire, beads and florist's wire.

1 Cut the shape of the handbag in florist's foam – I modelled mine on a vintage evening bag. Leave the foam to soak in water, then let it drain for two hours so that it won't drip.

2 Wrap the bag in chicken wire to hold its shape. Make a handle from beads strung on florist's wire or a piece of ribbon – anything that catches your eye. Attach the handle to the chicken-wire frame with florist's wire.

3 Cut the flower stems to about 2.5cm (1in) in length and strip them of foliage. Cut the stems at an angle to create a larger surface area for taking up water and make it easier to insert the pointed tips into the foam.

4 Push the roses into the foam to completely cover the bag.

5 Spray the roses with gold florist's paint. Then, if you want to, add two tiny rose buds threaded on florist's wire to create a clasp.

11

china

CHINA

WHEN I FIRST began my research into the origins of flowers and plants, I soon realized how important a role China had played. I had no idea how many of the garden plants that we assume to be native species actually began life in China. Not only do an enormous number of them originate there, but the Chinese have also been responsible for developing new varieties; as early as the fourth century they were producing different types of chrysanthemums, Chinese lanterns (*Physalis*), quince, hibiscus and peach blossom.

Tassels of purple wisteria flowers hugging the front of town houses in spring are a familiar sight in the West, yet it may come as a surprise to learn that the first plant wasn't imported from China to Europe until 1818. Forsythia is another Chinese original, but it grows almost wild in Britain, where it flourishes in the rather unpredictable climate, especially in over-grown gardens where it is left unpruned and unchecked.

Flowers hold a special significance for the Chinese, particularly at their New Year celebrations. The Chinese New Year is governed by the lunar calendar rather than the western version, so the date when it falls varies from year to year, although it is always somewhere between late January and mid-February. In Chinese cities around the world, flower fairs are set up on the 26th day of the last moon and run until the eve of the next new year. Taking a stroll through the fair buying flowers is a popular way of spending the last day of the old year.

Peach blossom plays a significant role in China's heritage, as the peach itself is a symbol of long life and a talisman against evil. Many families used to hang a spray above the front door to keep evil spirits away, although nowadays you are more likely to see peach blossom taken indoors and used as decoration. Blossom in general symbolizes life, growth and prosperity to the Chinese, and if a peach tree in a garden blooms at New Year, the year ahead is bound to be a good one for the household. Peonies, on the other hand, mean love and affection and indicate beauty; bright red peonies are the most favoured. Known as 'flowers of riches and honour', they are supposed to bring good fortune.

There are fantastic, uncompromising colour contrasts to be found in China, and two, in particular, stick in my mind: the black, white and red colour palette, which I consider industrial, functional and practical, and the riotous and altogether more extravagant and opulent colour combination of hot reds and pinks with clashing oranges and yellows.

__Right__ This pretty arrangement of red carnations in traditional white rice bowls creates a special occasion out of a simple Chinese meal. I've placed a small square of pre-soaked florist's foam in each bowl to hold the flowers in place, and then pushed cut-down carnation stems in around the edge of the foam at an angle pointing outwards. A central upright carnation creates the final dome-shaped effect, like a bowl piled high with noodles.
__Previous page, left__ On the label of this tin of lychees the dull pink skin of the fruit has been enhanced to a lurid unrealistic shade of red, a typically Chinese way of exaggerating colour to make something more appealing.
__Previous page, right__ Displaying a single vivid red carnation in a white rice bowl makes a bold and striking colour statement.

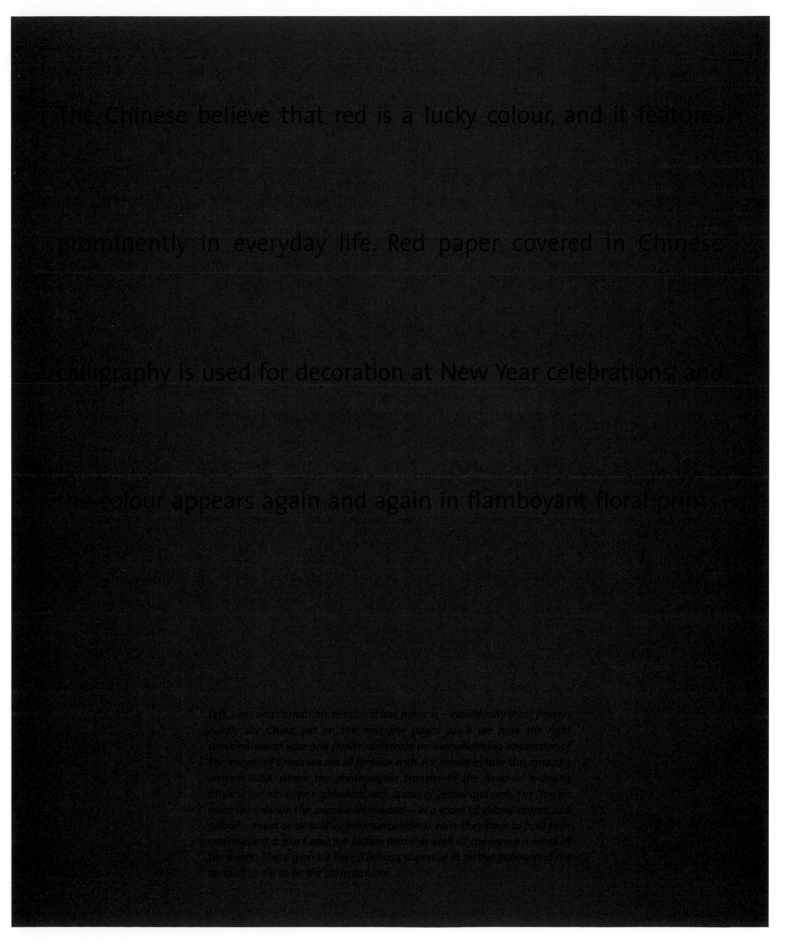

The Chinese believe that red is a lucky colour, and it features

prominently in everyday life. Red paper covered in Chinese

calligraphy is used for decoration at New Year celebrations, and

the colour appears again and again in flamboyant floral prints.

Left. Lilies and rantuntlons, bergamot and hibiscus – individually these flowers hardly say China, yet on the next few pages you'll see how the right combination of vase and flower can create an overwhelming impression of the images of China we are all familiar with. For example take this amazing ceramic vase, where the photographic transfer of the head of a young Chinese girl has been highlighted with glazes of yellow and pink. The flowers need to continue the oriental theme and – in a room of strong shapes and colours – must be as bold as their surroundings. Here they have to hold their own against a black and red picture frame as well as conveying a sense of the exotic. These gloriosa lilies (Gloriosa superba) in festive yellow and red seemed to me to be the perfect choice.

INDUSTRIAL CHIC

To capture the essence of industrial China, I've restricted the colours in this arrangement to red, black and white (and green, of course). I've already mentioned that red is a lucky colour in China, but there is also a great deal of symbolism attached to it. Red represents yang, or the male element – the sun, fire, summer, activity and the south. It is associated with vitality and passion and is the colour of happiness. Black has a special significance, too. It represents yin, or the female element – the moon, water, winter, rejuvenation and the north. But it is also a colour in daily life, from the high gloss of black lacquerware to hard-wearing clothing and acres of newsprint. Combined, red and black create balance and harmony.

For a real utilitarian look I've wrapped the vases in pages from a Chinese newspaper and held them in place with thin red rubber bands to continue the colour theme. The vases have been filled with bergamot and hibiscus; although these flowers are not exclusive to China, they combine to create the strong red impact that I was looking for. The large brightly coloured hibiscus has a fragile beauty that is enhanced to perfection by the colourful firework-like clusters of bergamot buds.

1 Choose two cylindrical vases of unequal height by similar diameter.

2 Neatly cut out a section of Chinese newspaper to the height of each container and wrap it around the outside, keeping the edges of the paper flush with the rim and base of the vase. Hold the newspaper in place with a couple of red rubber bands.

3 Prepare the flower stems by cutting them at an angle to maximize the uptake of water. Strip the lower leaves from the stems to prevent them from rotting under water.

4 Half-fill the vases with water. Arrange the hibiscus stems in the smaller vase and the bergamot in the taller.

Australia

KOALA

DESIGNED IN AUSTRALIA

australia

a USTRALIA IS FAST establishing itself as an innovator and leader in architecture, interior design and food. One element that unites these categories and what I always associate with Australia, is light. I don't just mean light in the sense of brightness and illumination, but also in the sheer light-heartedness of spirit – the open-spaced freshness of the architecture, which allows the maximum amount of light into the home, the clean lines of the furniture, the fresh raw ingredients in the kitchen and restaurants, combined with a spirit of adventure; and, finally, the climate that makes an outdoor lifestyle a reality.

I've had the great pleasure of working with many Antipodeans as they've made their youthful pilgrimages around the world. Somehow I feel there is a lightness to their soul, as if the sunlight they are used to has left an indelible stamp on their personalities. Australians are always upbeat, positive and enthusiastic about all they encounter.

I decided to use strong colour for my designs to evoke Australia's climate and wide open spaces. Like a dash of lime juice that gives a zing to the palate, strong colour creates a sense of energy and vitality.

The bold shapes of the containers echo the lines of the modern architecture, and the accessories – natural or man-made – add a sense of innovation. The flowers themselves are tough and 'masculine'. They're the kind of plants gardeners like to refer to as 'architectural', and when you look at the tall brazen stems of the bird-of-paradise flower you know exactly what they mean. The ingredients for the following designs and the ways in which they are combined enhance one another in colour and shape. The displays are simple in format, made in a few minutes, yet they achieve a sculptural significance. These are uncomplicated designs that enhance the clean lines of the interiors. Who needs fuss when life needs living?

Left Oblong glass tanks form a line down the centre of a table. The raw amethyst rocks piled into each container are a reminder that Australia is a country rich in minerals and resources. Their colour also works well with the lilac wall behind and the allium flowers, which are well on the way to turning into seedheads. If you don't want to invest in the amethyst rocks (although they're not massively expensive), there are plenty of cheaper alternatives – purple shells, marbles or even coloured gravel would all give a similar effect. The allium stems have been cut very short so that the seed heads balance on the edge of the containers. The look is incredibly simple and quick to achieve, falling easily within the five-minute flower-arranging rule. Alliums are not native Australian plants but, combined with the rocks in this display, they conjure up an arresting image of the arid outback.

Previous page, left A souvenir dishcloth featuring many people's favourite image of Australia – the koala bear.

Previous page, right A rosette from an echeveria, a tough succulent plant, sits on a map of Australia, the burnt withered edges of the plant echoing the edges of the coastline. Succulents such as these are well adapted to survive in harsh dry conditions. Their thick fleshy leaves conserve water and the waxy covering stops them drying out completely. Even the rosette formation of tightly packed overlapping leaves is another way of the plant reducing water loss.

Cubist Colours *(left)*

These ceramic cube vases have a 1970s retro feel. Here I've stacked them but you could use them singly or line several of them along a surface. Filling each cube with neon-bright dahlias has something of a retro feel about it, too; dahlias were big garden favourites from the 1950s onwards. Now they are available commercially from spring through to autumn, in flower-head sizes that range from 5–20cm (2–8in). The variation in colour combinations is vast, from the purest white to the darkest burgundy, with everything in between. All you'll need for this design is a block of florist's foam, approximately 2cm (¾in) deep, for each vase.

1 In the base of each vase sit a block of pre-soaked florist's foam.
2 Cut the dahlia stems so that they are about 3–4cm (1¼–1½in) long.
3 Push 2cm (¾in) of stem into the foam, arranging the flowers precisely in a grid-like way for a neat flat surface.
4 Top up with water daily.

Right *Four allium stems catch the eye displayed in a cylindrical glass vase. To make this design work a little harder, I've pushed the stems through purple nylon tubing. Don't ask me what this tubing was for originally; I found it in a wholesale haberdashers, alongside more conventional lace and ribbons. Make sure that the stems are free of foliage before pushing them gently through the lengths of tubing. This shouldn't be too difficult to do because the tubes are quite flexible and the allium stems are fairly rigid.*

Right Strelitzia, or bird-of-paradise flowers as they are commonly named for obvious reasons, are an incredibly good buy because they are so long lasting. The 'beak' of the flower holds numerous buds that open in succession and you can gently pull the next flower free from the stack of sticky buds as the previous flower dies. The flowers are a striking orange and purple in colour and feel fleshy to the touch. The stems are free of foliage and grow to approximately 1.2m (4ft) high. They rise up from a huge rosette of spear-like leaves, which are greyish-green in colour and thick and fleshy. Strelitzia practically grows wild in Australia, making it an obvious choice for flower designs. Placed randomly in large vases of orange and black, which have been spaced unevenly on a bare floor, the flowers have a very dramatic effect.

AUSTRALIA

This page *Banksia and grevillea are native to Australia. It's easy to see how these robust flowers survive the arid climates that dominate parts of the country. Just look at the thick woody stems, harsh brittle foliage and textural wiry tendrils that make up the large dense flower heads. I've used them in cylindrical glass vases with their stems pushed down into white sand, so that they resemble showcase specimens. You need just a few for maximum effect. The yellow flower in the central vase is the grevillea, flanked by two banksia. Use florist's water vials to prolong the life of the flowers, or leave them to dry.*
Right *A large glass tank has been filled with water-absorbing gel, a substance used by gardeners for pots or hanging baskets to improve the water-retaining properties of compost. If you mix the powder with water, it swells to a see-through jelly-like substance that looks fabulous in clear glass vases. I've used it here to suspend seashells and coral. Resting on the surface are white hydrangea flower heads, representing breaking waves.*

Left *Neon-yellow calla lilies have been bound with Perspex (Plexiglas) bangles and laid flat on a table surface. Calla lilies will easily survive an evening left out of water but, as an alternative display, you could stand them upright in a Perspex cube vase, supporting them vertically with coloured gravel in the base, or simply place them in a tall narrow vase.*

It's possible that I may be stating the obvious here, but I do want to emphasize the importance of all the design ingredients working together – vase, flowers and surroundings. Clean, modern textures and materials, such as Perspex, used in modern architectural surroundings need simple and uncomplicated flowers. The understated elegance of the lily stems and the bright cone-shaped flowers are a perfect fit with the other elements.

holland

V ISITING THE DUTCH flower auctions for the first time, I was immediately struck by the sheer vastness of it all – from the huge characterless grey concrete halls, devoid of sunlight yet alive with the scent and colour of flowers, to the thousands and thousands, if not millions, of stems that pass through the auctions every day. There seemed to be no end to the row upon row of automated trolleys stacked with boxes and buckets of blooms, all awaiting their moment of glory. Dutch flower auctions are a stressful business. Several hundred buyers sit watching two enormous 'clocks'. These indicate the quantity of stems available, the grower, stem length and various other details. The hand of the clock swings up to hit a price marked on the face and this is where the buyer's dilemma kicks in: press the buzzer too soon and pay a high price or wait for the hand to drop and miss an opportunity altogether. The Dutch take flowers very seriously. Holland is home to the largest flower auctions in the world, handling home-grown produce as well as acting as a distribution centre for flowers flown in from around the globe. Once they've been bought 'from the clocks', the distributors then resell them to wholesale markets, supermarkets and smaller retailers.

Holland not only grows the largest proportion of the world's flowers, it is also influential in developing new varieties for retail. Growers and seed developers are advised on trends several years in advance by the same forecasters who advise fashion and lifestyle companies. It is no accident that amazing lime-green chrysanthemum blooms are suddenly on sale just as an East-meets-West trend sweeps the globe or that a chocolate-coloured anthurium becomes available when brown leather is in vogue.

The Dutch love affair and obsession with flowers dates back to at least 1634 when 'Tulip Fever' took hold. Fortunes were made and lost as people gambled their homes, their businesses, their all, on buying and selling tulip bulbs. Prices spiralled crazily upwards until the inevitable crash in 1637.

As Holland is probably best known for bulb flowers, I have concentrated on using tulips, narcissi, hyacinths and amaryllis (*Hippeastrum*) for the displays in this section. All of them are available in abundance in winter and spring but with an ever-lengthening season, and tulips seem to be on sale pretty much throughout the year now.

Flowers are big business in Holland, with the population as a whole spending more money per head on them than in any other country.

Left *To make this arrangement you'll need a large fish bowl or vase with a 5cm (2in) layer of gravel in the base, colour-coordinated to the shade of your tulips. Add a shallow amount of water. Leave the tulips out of water for an hour or so before placing them in the container, so that their stems become flaccid and flexible, making them easier to bend to the contours of the bowl.*
Previous pages *I love tulips, particularly parrot tulips with their brushstrokes of colour on raggedy petals that deepen and grow as the flowers open. I find the squeaky sound of the fleshy stems pleasing and the waxy texture of the petals appealing, like wax crayons or the wax covering on Dutch cheese.*

A Modern Old Master

This arrangement is inspired by the Dutch old masters of the 1700s, who captured the finest of details of flowers and nature in their paintings. I've given the flowers a modern-day twist by using an urn flocked with bright orange velvet and, rather than a selection of flowers, I've used only two.

There are many different varieties of narcissi available. The bright yellow and orange-centred one here is 'Craig Ford'; the orange centre picks out the colour of the urn and the crown imperial lilies (*Fritillaria imperialis*). Instead of narcissi, you could try pinks or sweet William – flowers with rounded heads will mass together nicely. Instead of fritillaria, try pink delphiniums or lilies, toning the colour of the flowers with your container.

It was traditional for Dutch painters to include insects among the flowers within their paintings, and I've attempted to honour this tradition in my design by fixing two beautiful scientific specimens of beetles onto the urn with double-sided adhesive tape.

1. Mass the stems of narcissi into a dome. Do this by holding a few stems in one hand and gradually add more and more stems in a spiral around them. As the spiral grows, the angle of the flowers will change from upright to 90 degrees, to form the dome shape. Have some raffia or string to hand so that you can tie the stems in place to keep the dome intact. If necessary, cut the stems so that the flowers rest on the rim of the urn.

2. Insert the taller stems of fritillaria through the dome; they will be supported by the framework of narcissi.

JUNGLE PRINTS *(above)*

It is essential to look at your surroundings and be led by them when choosing flowers or plants. In this contemporary room the 1970s sofa plays a major role, as do the glass surfaces and clean white walls. There's nothing shy and retiring about the decor – it is strong and bold, and the flowers need to hold their own within it. For this display, I've used two amaryllis bulbs, which contribute their own beautiful shape and texture, and placed them in a vase filled with layers of white sand, rich dark compost and gravel to mirror the pattern, texture and colour of the sofa.

1 Choose an over-sized glass vase that will make its own statement.

2 Mix the textures by layering the sand, compost and gravel. To create the layers, tilt the vase and pour in the sand, then gradually tilt it the other way as you add the compost, before holding it level to add the gravel.

3 Buy potted bulbs, remove the pots and add the bulbs with the compost intact. Surround the bulbs with more gravel. Even before the flowers open, the emerging emerald-green spears of the stems look amazing.

Right I love hyacinth bulbs, possibly more than the flowers, although I admit their fragrance is hard to beat. They are a wonderful colour and the texture of their skin is like paper; in the blue varieties the skin is an iridescent purple. I love the white tendril-like roots emerging from the base of the bulb and the pointed fleshy green leaves that pierce the top. I've planted these bulbs in traditional wooden seed trays, lined with plastic to hold the compost, then added a layer of crushed shells dyed lime green, which picks up the colour of the foliage and creates a clean contemporary mood. The result is a mix of old and new that would sit easily in a country location or city apartment.

morocco

C REATING AN IMPRESSION of a country is a challenge, especially with somewhere like Morocco where the influences come at you from every angle, from the religious chants that echo through the streets at sunrise to the noise and chaos of the busy souks. What shines through, though, is the passion and intensity of the way of life, the frantic activity in the streets and squares long after night has fallen.

But there is another, gentler side to Morocco. May is the month in which the headily fragrant roses are harvested. Whole families comb the hedgerows and vast rose fields in the south of the country, removing the flower heads and dropping them into baskets or shawls tied to their backs. The day's work complete, mules transport the harvest to small village factories where the heaps of blooms are pressed for their oil. It takes an unbelievable amount of petals, vast mountains of them, to yield a scant litre of precious extract. The raw product is sold worldwide to perfume houses and to the food industry. Morocco also manufactures some of its own rose products within the country, typically rose water, cosmetic lotions and potions, as well as rose-flavoured Turkish delight.

Rose petals are used freely to decorate restaurant tables and bedrooms in hotels and villas. I've even heard tales of rose petals strewn from balconies as guests enter a hotel. Can you imagine anything more divine?

In the end, it just seemed right to me to focus on roses for my interpretation of Morocco. The depth and range of rose colours available to us is quite incredible, and I've chosen intense shades that capture the mood, colour and textures that are undoubtedly Morocco.

To capture the essence of Morocco, I felt I had to create something that was passionate and romantic, something that appealed to the senses.

Left *Candles and lanterns play a prominent role in Moroccan life, and for this design I've displayed deep burgundy candles and vessels of the same shade in an assortment of shapes and sizes against a background of scarlet and white mosaic tiles. A mosaic pattern made with squares of rose petals in scarlet, pink and white, stripped from the flower heads, covers the tabletop. This may seem extravagant, yet it doesn't have to be. As it is obviously a decoration that lasts for one evening only, there is no need to buy top-quality roses. Visit a market stall or street vendor and buy flowers that are perhaps slightly past their best, fully open and inexpensive. To keep the edges of the mosaic well defined, mark out a grid first on the tabletop using tape or string.*
Previous page, left *Saffron-coloured leather slippers lined with plastic conceal blocks of pre-soaked florist's foam holding multicoloured rose heads. The roses are a type of rose, known as 'Henri Matisse' or 'Zebra'.*
Previous page, right *'Ecstasy' roses in one of the darkest shades imaginable. Unusually for commercially grown roses, they have a wonderful scent.*

ROSE GARLAND *(left)*

Decorate a candelabrum with roses for an indulgent display. Use garlands of rose petals strung together on lengths of coloured florist's wire. As with the mosaic design on page 94, it's not necessary to use first-rate flowers.

1 Cut a length of wire – these garlands are approximately 1m (3ft) long – and make a knot at one end. As a rough guide, you'll need around ten roses per 50cm (18in) of wire.

2 Very gently, so as not to bruise or tear them, twist the flower heads to release the petals.

3 Just like using a needle and thread, pierce the centre of the petals with the wire, pushing them down to the knot. Continue until the wire is full.

4 Knot the free end of the wire and twist it into a loop to hang.

Above Mint tea is on offer everywhere in Morocco. Bunches of pungent fresh leaves are steeped in boiling water, then sweetened generously with large crystals of amber sugar. Gold-adorned tea glasses are used in daily life as cups but they can also double up as candleholders or vases. Be generous with the number of glasses you use, lining them down the centre of a table or along a bar counter or shelf. Fill the glasses with water and cut the bunches of mint so that the ball of leaves sits on the rim. To echo the gold decoration on the tea glasses, insert metallic paper leaves among the fresh foliage – I used confectioner's leaves for decorating cakes and attached them to thin wires – they will shimmer beautifully in candlelight at the table. You can find bunches of mint at greengrocers or supermarkets, or you can buy pots from the garden centre and cut down the stems. You may even come across pots of genuine Moroccan mint, which tends to have distinctive crinkly leaves.

MOROCCO

SPICE MOUNTAINS

Walk through the labyrinths of alleyways or into the market places of Morocco and all of your senses are bombarded from every direction. Music and the calls of the street vendors, incense blended with the scent of leather and woollen carpets – and spices, more spices than you could ever imagine, poured into tall pyramids on woven metal dishes and finishing in a pinnacle, just like the surrounding mountains.

Market-place mountains of spice are the inspiration for these table decorations, which I've placed on engraved Moroccan platters. Choose roses in shades of amber, coral and saffron to imitate the real thing. If you can, use spray roses because they're smaller and easier to work with to define the conical shape. You'll also need a large block of florist's foam.

1 Cut off all the flower heads, at an angle, leaving a 2.5cm (1in) stem on each flower and remove any foliage.

2 Carve a conical shape from the foam using a knife. Soak it in water, then leave it to drain for an hour before placing it on the platter.

3 Add the roses, working from the bottom upwards. Start by using the largest flower heads, encircling the 'mountain' and gradually working upwards. Save the smallest buds to make the mountain peak.

japan

d ELICATE CANDY-PINK cherry blossom is a national symbol in Japan. You see it every day, on packaging for all sorts of things, from green tea to chewing gum. It's used to garnish food in expensive restaurants, while plastic imitations are tied to lamp-posts to decorate the street. Cherry blossom designs are woven into intricate silk kimonos, and painted on lacquered containers and vases. In spring the whole nation celebrates the cherry blossom festivals, a tradition dating back to at least the seventh century. Families head for the park and picnic beneath the cherry trees, consuming copious amounts of sake to mark the occasion.

We're all familiar with the heavily laden branches of cherry blossom and the contrast between the gnarled and twisted grey bark and the pendulous pink flowers delicately strung on green stems. After a few glorious days of blossom the petals scatter on the breeze like confetti, leaving the fruit to develop. The cherry blossom grown commercially for florists, though, is a completely different animal. It has thin stretched stems that are greenish-brown, with small round blooms hugging the stem.

If you want to create a structured arrangement, commercial cherry blossom with its flexible stems is far easier to work with and – like any commercially grown flower – lasts longer. I don't think it has quite the charm of nature's creation, but it certainly has its uses.

The chrysanthemum is another flower we tend to think of as being typically Japanese, although it was actually introduced to Japan from China. Buddhist monks took plants there in the fourth century, and the flowers quickly became as popular as cherry blossom. Centuries later the British took the chrysanthemum to heart, too. The Chrysanthemum Society of 1846 promoted the cultivation of hundreds of different varieties, which were displayed at regional and national shows.

I feel very nostalgic about chrysanthemums, perhaps because they dominated the gardens in Britain during the 1950s and 60s. They remind me of my grandfather, carrying them home carefully wrapped in newspaper, freshly cut from his allotment. It's a vivid example of how time and place affect our perception of flowers – how chrysanthemums can be viewed as traditionally British as well as traditionally Japanese. Change the setting and surroundings and you change a flower's image completely.

Japan is an amazing blend of contradictions, where a reverence for tradition and a passion for all things kitsch sit comfortably side by side.

Right *In this display I've mixed two strong cultural references: the delicate stems of traditional cherry blossom and fluorescent-pink wax-covered apples. This juxtaposition of the old and the new, the real and the artificial, is something that you are reminded of constantly in Japan. The overall look is contemporary, dictated by the choice of vases: a large glass sphere with a tall cylinder stood inside. Cherry blossom stems are pliable so they can be wound around the inside of the sphere fairly easily. Cut at least 2cm (¾in) off the bottom of each stem, at an angle, and slit each stem vertically by the same amount to maximize water uptake; make sure the cut ends are underwater.*
Previous pages *The contrasting images of Japan: a sprig of cherry blossom and fluorescent-pink, wax-coated apples, with a 'Hello Kitty' sticker.*

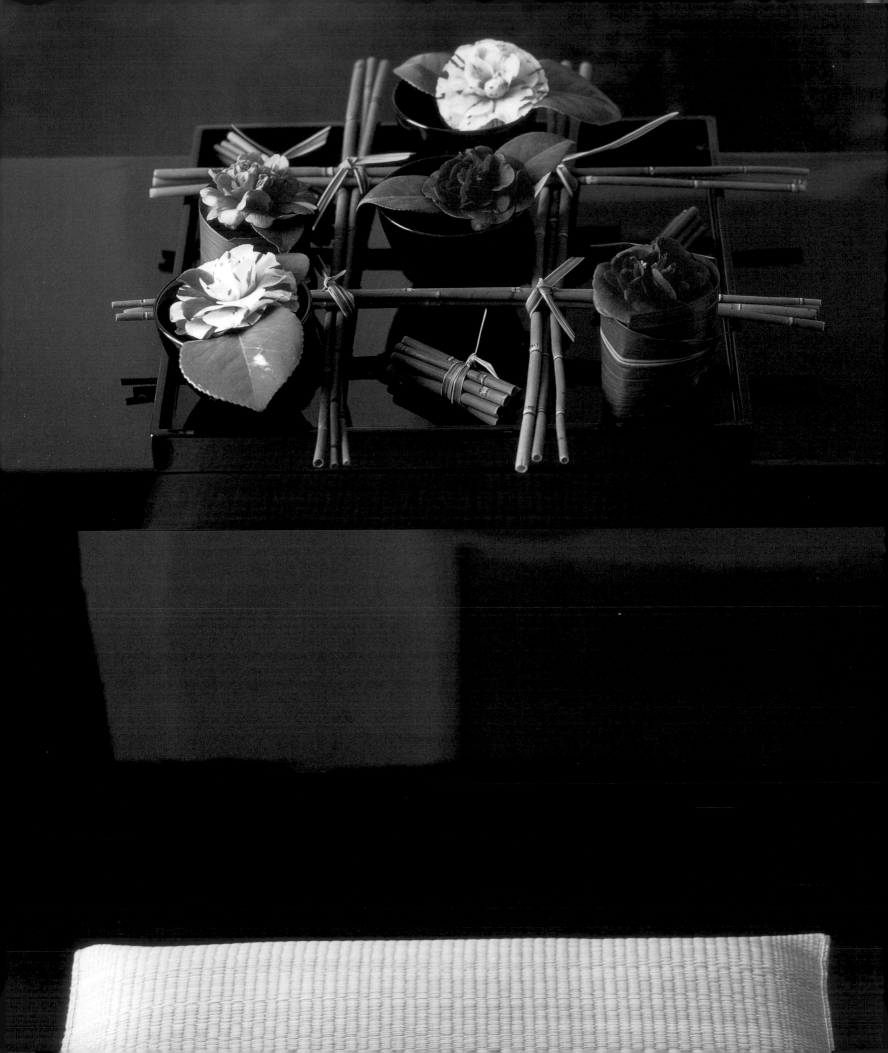

FUSING FLOWERS AND FOOD

By looking at the art of the sushi chef who creates beautifully crafted jewels of food, I came up with the idea of a Japanese bento, or lunch, box, featuring 'sushi' camellias wrapped in aspidistra leaves. Bento vary in style from the humble plastic workman's lunch boxes at railway stations to lacquered wooden boxes with ornate chopsticks to match. Typically they are divided into six or nine compartments, each holding rice, vegetables, pickles and meat or fish. For this display I've used a bamboo grid to represent the compartments. You'll also need a shallow dish or lacquered tray for the bento box, fresh bamboo or snake grass, China grass, aspidistra leaves, camellia flowers, florist's foam, florist's wire and double-sided tape.

1 To make the grid, first make four bundles of three or four fresh bamboo stems or snake grass bound together with wire. The grid needs to be as large as your bento box, with at least a 2.5cm (1in) overlap all around. Lay the bundles across the bento box in a grid shape and bind the stems in place with wire where they cross each other. Disguise the wire with China grass and place the finished grid on the box.

2 For the 'sushi', cut a circle of florist's foam about 5cm (2in) in diameter and 2.5cm (1in) deep. Soak the foam and leave it to drain. Cut the stem of an open camellia flower to 5cm (2in) in length. Push it into the foam.

3 Cut off the stem and base of an aspidistra leaf to make it more flexible. Wrap it around the foam circle, leaving the pointed tip of the leaf visible. Hold it in place with double-sided tape. Tie China grass around the leaf.

4 Make up several wrapped flowers in the same way, using different coloured blooms. Alternate them with short bundles of bamboo tied together with China grass. If camellias are out of season, substitute peonies, carnations or roses. Try varying the design; halved limes, for example, look fantastic interspersed between the flowers.

BAMBOO AND CHRYANTHEMUMS *(left)*

Many chrysanthemum varieties have a Japanese name: 'Fuji' is pink and white; 'Tokyo', white and yellow. However, the green oriental-style flowers I've used here are known as 'Shamrock', for obvious reasons, but they work perfectly well with this Japanese theme. I've teamed them with stems of giant bamboo, filling the fireplace. They would look just as good on the mantelpiece, along a counter or bar top or, if the bamboo stems were left really tall, standing on the floor in an entrance hall.

1 Cut stems of giant bamboo to different lengths, just above a joint. At this point there is a natural division within the bamboo that can be used to form the base of the 'vase' and hold a block of florist's foam.

2 Cut the florist's foam so that it will sit below the top of the bamboo 'vase' without being visible. Soak the foam in water and leave it to drain.

3 Cut the chrysanthemum stems at a sharp angle, leaving approximately 5cm (2in) of stem behind each flower head. Push the stems into the foam so that the bottom of each flower head is level with the top of the bamboo. Use one, two or three flowers per bamboo, depending on their size.

This page Camellias figure large in Japanese history, both illustrating ancient manuscripts and decorating porcelain and lacquerware. White camellias are traditional at weddings where they symbolize a long life. They also come in shades of pink and red, and different varieties have different forms, some reminiscent of roses or peonies, others opening out as generously as water lilies.

Above and right *Forsythia, originally from the Orient but now grown all over the world, flowers in the garden in early spring, providing one of the first splashes of colour. In the West, forsythia is often teamed with daffodils or narcissi that bloom around the same time. Students of ikebana, the Japanese art of flower arranging, prefer to use it alone, to appreciate the beauty of its delicate star-like flowers. Used against a black lacquer background, as here, the 1.8m (6ft) tall straight branches make a dramatic vertical stripe of colour. The upright form also lends a minimalist air to the arrangement.*

america

y ES, I HAVE to admit it, I am a dreamer. I can completely immerse myself in the history of a building or place, imagining the people who have lived there or visited, what they were wearing, and who they were with. Maybe I've watched too many old movies but, oh, the romance of it all. I feel that there has to be a little bit of dreaming involved when you're working in any field of design; you must be able to connect with your materials and understand the mood or image that's inspired you.

North America is an incredible country, with each state having a unique history, feel and style. Here I've concentrated on just one aspect of this diversity – vintage Hollywood and the movies. I need you to imagine smart hotels, luxurious luggage, bellboys, room service, martinis and furs to get you in the mood. That's exactly what I did when I chose the flowers and foliage for the following designs. The result is pure old-time glamour.

It's impossible to capture the diversity that is America in just a few pages so, instead, I've focused on what sums up America to me – glamour.

Left *An urn of clipped pine needles holds a bouquet of magnolia leaves and white amaryllis at a hotel reception desk. A fake fur bow tied around the 'waist' of the urn below the rim imitates a mink stole, complementing the suede-like texture of the underside of the magnolia leaves. Fur also trims the base of the urn. The overall effect is one of understated opulence.*

To make the urn, I moulded a frame from chicken wire by bending and shaping the sheet of wire, then binding the edges together with florist's wire. I then pushed 'fingers' of pine foliage into the wire and trimmed them until I achieved a recognizable urn shape. The magnolia stems, with their lower leaves removed, have been cut to a sharp point and their stems pushed into pre-soaked florist's foam, placed in the urn on a lining of polythene. I inserted some magnolia leaves with their textural undersides uppermost to increase the sense of opulence; others I laid flat so that the leaves formed a collar around the rim of the urn. Then I made holes in the foam and pushed the soft amaryllis stems gently into the centre of the display. The fake fur trims were the final sumptuous additions.

Previous page, left *A star-shaped cake tin painted blue holds pre-soaked florist's foam and heads of roses sprayed with blue florist's paint. The stems of the roses are cut short so that the heads are level with the rim of the tin. Placed on sequined stripes, the effect is glitzy razzmatazz – it reminds me of a baton-twirling, high-kicking cheerleader.*

Previous page, right *A giant martini glass, more than 1m (3ft) tall, makes a magnificent impact as a table centre or an entrance display. It's filled with water and tiny glass 'bubbles', which are available from florists, to reflect the light. A stem of phalaenopsis orchids arches languidly over the side of the glass while individual blooms decorate the base. The impression is one of ultimate exquisite luxury – something that all of us would probably love to experience at least once in our lives.*

WRIST CORSAGE (above)

To make these romantic wrist corsages I've attached flowers to a diamanté bracelet and to a bracelet of pink pearls. You'll need florist's wire in two gauges – very fine and regular – florist's tape, plus your chosen flowers.

1 For the left-hand corsage, cut the flowers of green dendrobium orchids from the main stem and wind fine florist's wire around each flower base to create an artificial stem. Bind this with tape to cover up any scratchy ends. Hook the flexible wire stem between the segments of the bracelet.

2 The right-hand corsage is made up of two roses: pink 'Bianca Candy' and lilac 'Stirling Silver'. Cut the stem of the 'Bianca Candy' rose about 1cm (½in) below the calyx. Push a length of the regular wire up through the stem and into the head to create a false stem. Remove some of the outer petals.

3 Twist the petals off the 'Stirling Silver' rose and wire a selection of them individually with fine florist's wire cut into lengths by making a small stitch across the back of each petal about a third of the way from the tip. Pull the wire through so that one 'leg' is about two thirds longer than the other. Hold the stitch and fold down the wire, twisting the longer end around the shorter one and scrunching up the petal base to make a stem.

4 Lay the wired petals around the rose centre so that they overlap. Tape the wire petal stems onto the central wire with florist's tape. Entwine the stem around the bracelet. Now you're ready for the ball!

Right Black-and-white movies, where the bellboy delivers flowers in a glossy box with a satin bow to the heroine's hotel room, were the inspiration behind this gift of green cymbidium orchids. There's an immediate impression of expense and romance attached to these flowers that still exists today.

CASINO ROYALE

To re-create the atmosphere of a 1960s James-Bond style casino – suave handsome men and glamorous jet-set women, with big hair and a passion for fast cars, playing blackjack and roulette – the flowers need to look the part and impress. I've used a vase sculpted from a huge block of ice. (Catering companies specializing in ice sculptures are quite a thriving business – but if you can't track one down, go for a narrow glass vase instead.) The vase stands tall in the centre of the table, holding a tiered cascade of arum lilies. The way the light reflects in the ice, the frosted texture and the very fact that the display is so temporary creates an illusion of sheer indulgence and excess. As well as approximately 31 stems of arum lilies – the number will depend on the size of the vase and how many stems are needed for a snug fit – you'll need some clear tape.

1 Bind the stems of the top tier of six flowers together a little way below their heads with clear tape. Make the stems all the same length, cutting them straight across for stability.

2 Position the middle tier of ten flowers around the stems of the top tier so that the flowers conceal the tape wrapped around the flowers above. Then bind the stems of the middle tier together with tape. Cut the stems straight across, lining them up with the ends of the stems in the top tier.

3 Repeat with 15 stems for the bottom tier, cutting the stems straight across and lining them up with the stems of the two other tiers. There is no need to bind the stems together. Place the three tiers in the vase. All the stems should line up and touch the bottom of the vase.

4 Add water.

CHRISTMAS PARCELS *(left)*

A display of gifts stacked up on a table could be used to mark many different occasions simply by changing the colour of the flowers. Here I've used rich velvety red 'Grand Prix' roses in three different-sized glass cube vases with a silver mirror finish to celebrate Christmas. Alternatively, you could use plain glass cubes and decorate them by spraying the inner surface with metallic paint. You'll also need florist's foam and ribbon.

1 Cut a cube of florist's foam so that it sits 5cm (2in) below the rim of the vase. Cut the rose stems, at a sharp angle, to about 2.5cm (1in) in length.

2 Push the roses into the pre-soaked foam in a grid formation for a neat square finish, leaving the heads just showing over the rim.

3 Tie a generous bow of ribbon parcel-style around the vase.

WREATHED IN LEAVES *(right)*

For this door wreath I've used magnolia leaves. Long lasting out of water, they have an incredible rich brown 'suede' underside. A length of mock mink fur, tied into a bow, adds the finishing touch. You'll also need a wire wreath frame, sphagnum moss, reel wire or string and strong florist's wire.

1 Cover the frame with moss by binding it in place with wire or string.

2 Make 'hairpins' by bending short lengths of florist's wire into shape.

3 Cut individual magnolia leaves from the branches. Starting on the outside edge of the wreath, layer one leaf on top of another; they should face the same direction with the 'suede' side uppermost. Secure the base of each leaf with a hairpin, concealing each hairpin with the tip of the next leaf. Encircle the base completely. Repeat the process for the inside edge.

4 Add the central line of leaves on top of the wreath in the same way.

5 Tie the fake fur into a bow and bind it in place with wire.

6 Fix a hanging loop made out of strong wire at the top of the wreath.

Right Behind the scenes in an exclusive hotel, a room service trolley stands abandoned in the corridor. The gift posy on the trolley is a mass of tight rose buds, spiralled into a dome shape. There's quite an art to making such a posy. You need to hold the first rose upright and wrap string around the binding point. Add the second stem at a slight angle and bind that in position. Rotate the bunch in your hand as you continue to add more stems. Some of the rose buds in this posy have been brushed with glue and dusted with iridescent glitter, while square-cut diamanté stones have been wired into place between the flowers. A white satin ribbon covers the binding point of the spiralled stems. This would be the perfect presentation bouquet for a VIP or a bride's posy for a winter wedding.

india

INDIAN MARKETS ARE full of colour, sound and scent. Stalls are piled high with saris of every shade imaginable, and temptation lies all around, from the teetering heaps of jewel-encrusted shoes to racks of waistcoats embellished with scraps of mirror. Add to this the all-pervading scent from drifting clouds of incense and the tapping of the silversmiths and metalworkers, and you'll have some idea of the chaos, confusion and bright, bright colour that to me sums up India.

Flowers in India are used in the most imaginative and exuberant ways. At festivals images of the gods are garlanded with flowers and wheeled through the streets in decorated palanquins. The traditional art of rangoli, where courtyards, walls and thatched roofs are decorated with patterns, uses basketfuls of oleander, cosmos and chrysanthemum flowers to produce fleeting carpets and murals of petals.

To get into the spirit of India, think of the ever-popular Bollywood movies – melodramatic storylines, the flamboyant gestures of the actors and dancers, loud and frenzied music. The colours look as if they've been cranked up to boiling point. Think of Indian weddings, too. These stretch over several days, starting off slowly with hours devoted to adorning the bride, painting her hands and feet with henna, as she reclines on a day bed beneath a canopy of flowers. The ceremony is often quite literally staged before the real partying gets underway.

In my designs, I've used these images as starting points to capture the spirit of India but in a way that is practical and relevant to everyone.

Left and below *A traditional lattice-work tabletop holds clashing red and yellow roses and purple amaranthus in a grid-based pattern. The stems have been cut short and pushed into florist's vials, then dropped into the lattice. I've tucked some incense sticks, wired discreetly for stability, in among the flowers.*
Previous page, left *A fine and lacy hand-shaped stencil used to create a henna pattern on the body, with a marigold – a popular flower in India.*
Previous page, right *Paint pigments in the most intense colours.*

When I think of India, I immediately think colour – bright fuchsia-

pink colliding head on with vivid orange; saffron robes and

marigold flowers piled high in the market place; pyramids of

paint pigments in turquoise, sugar-pink and fluorescent green.

SHADES OF VELVET

There's something about flocked wallpaper that sums up the days of the Raj, not to mention the decor of your local Indian restaurant. I've used wallpaper offcuts and samples to wrap vases filled with celosia in shades of hot pink, ruby-red and mango, plus feathery amaranthus. The velvety flowers are a perfect match for the flocking on the wallpaper. You will need three square vases, wallpaper, double-sided tape and stems of celosia and amaranthus.

1 Lay the wallpaper out flat and cut off enough to wrap the vase. Make a double fold at one end to form a cuff.

2 Wrap the vase, joining the ends of the paper with double-sided tape. Fold and tape the wallpaper neatly over the base so that the vase sits flat. Leave the cuff end open for the flower stems.

3 Fill the vase with water and add the celosia and amaranthus. Mass the flower heads together, cutting the stems so that the heads rest on the cuff.

Right *The lotus is a sacred flower in India, featuring prominently in folklore and legend. In paintings and manuscripts Buddha is often depicted sitting on a lotus flower. The blooms have only recently become available as cut flowers in Western markets, now that methods have been developed to transport their delicate blooms safely. The flowers come in pinks, whites, purples and yellow, opening to a star-like shape to reveal the most incredible centre of stamens and to release their delicate rose-like scent. For this arrangement I've hidden small, narrow glass tumblers within stacks of Indian bangles. The tumblers are full of water and the lotus stems have been cut so that the flowers sit above the rim of the bracelets. Group them together for maximum impact – the more colour there is, the better.*

r

OSES, STOCKS, CARNATIONS, tuberose and lilies are all grown in Mexico for the cut-flower industry. They are fabulous flowers but they don't instantly summon up images of Mexico. I needed to add a sense of location, introducing colours and textures through containers, accessories and, of course, architecture, that created the effect I was looking for.

So just what is Mexican? What immediately says Mexico? My first thoughts were typical clichés: ponchos and sombreros, chilies and tequila. But when I sat down and did some research, other elements came into play.

I discovered that modern award-winning Mexican architecture and traditional Mexican festivals share the same exuberant bold colours. The simmering yellow, neon-pink, reds and purples of festive clothing inspired the interior palette of architect and landscape artist Luis Barragán. More subdued shades feature in the paintings of Frida Kahlo, while the vast public murals of her husband Diego Rivera, who brought art out into the streets, bring vibrant colour full circle again.

In daily life the same colours sing out from religious shrines adorned with mementoes and flowers, both fresh and plastic. Retablos, traditional folk paintings on pieces of tin, copper or wood, use vivid colour to represent images of the saints that decorate homes all over Mexico. The great November festival of the Day of the Dead, when families remember relatives who have died – as well as celebrating the continuity of life – sees graves decorated with flowers and ornaments. Cemeteries come alive with colour, graves are heaped typically with marigolds and chrysanthemums, and whole families bring picnics and spend the day feasting there.

I took a little inspiration from each of these, with inevitably the most important element being colour. For flowers I've concentrated mainly on the use of air plants (*Tillandsia*), cacti and succulents that thrive in the arid desert environment but survive equally well in European interiors.

Bold, exuberant colour is to be found everywhere in Mexico, in the city and the country, at traditional festivals and in modern art and architecture.

Right Miniature air plants, about 15cm (6in) apart, have been attached to long strands of red wire, twisted and knotted around the base of each plant. The wires are suspended from a door frame, acting as a screen, like an alternative to a traditional beaded door curtain. Air plants are so called because they don't need soil to survive – just a light misting of water from time to time will keep them going indefinitely.

Previous page, left A large cylindrical and very spiny cactus planted in a turquoise plastic bowl and surrounded with ochre sand. The sand highlights and exaggerates the golden spines of the cactus.

Previous page, right Packaging typical of the sort that surrounds and protects awesome branched cacti – just like those you see in Westerns – as they cross continents for export.

RED HOT AND FIERY *(right)*
A column of chili peppers, topped with a dome of flowers like a Carmen Miranda hat, creates a Latin-American riot of colour and texture. You'll need a cylindrical glass vase, a small plate that will fit snugly on top of the vase, florist's tape, florist's foam, cocktail sticks, plus a selection of chili peppers, a succulent plant, such as an echeveria, red carnations and roses.

This arrangement could be repeated using different ingredients to indicate inspiration from elsewhere in the world. Be guided by the season and location. Fill the vase with kumquats and a dome of orange flowers for an oriental effect; a column of star anise and cinnamon sticks topped with magnolia foliage and terracotta roses would look suitably autumnal.

1 Fill the vase with peppers – here I've used a glorious mixture of scarlet and yellow. Put the small plate on top of the vase.

2 Fix a block of pre-soaked florist's foam to the plate with florist's tape.

3 Cut the stems of the roses and carnations to approximately 6cm (2¼in) in length and push them into the foam to a depth of 3cm (1¼in).

4 Cut individual rosettes of leaves from the succulent. Push three or four cocktail sticks into the base of each rosette, then push these into the foam.

This page Sand and gravel in muted sun-baked colours has been used to surround small cacti repotted in tequila shot glasses. Tap the pot to release the cactus – always wear gardening gloves when handling cacti – and gently brush loose compost from the roots before repotting the plant in sand. A piece of driftwood painted a striking cobalt-blue completes the picture.

MEXICO

This page The colour red dominates daily life in Mexico, in everything from woven tapestry-type fabrics, garish plastic bowls and painted tin trays to the searingly hot chilies sold at street vendors' stalls. The same bright hue is present in geranium flowers (strictly speaking, pelargoniums), which flourish in hot countries like Mexico. For this arrangement I've simply cut stems from classic red geraniums and displayed them in an assortment of brightly decorated drinking glasses. The effect is instant.

Left Modern architecture in Mexico City mixes white with bold statements of colour. For my interpretation of this uncompromising use of colour with a desert theme, I've taken plastic washing-up bowls in a cross section of vivid colours and filled them in turn with sands in lurid shades. The bowls hold a mixture of cacti and succulents, still in their original pots but sunk into the sand so that the pots aren't visible. The effect is the complete opposite of subtle coordinating colours, and I love it. For a more permanent display, remove the cacti from their pots and replant them directly in the sand.

Colour is turned up high in Mexico. Nothing is bland or run-of-

the-mill, from the packaging and advertising for everyday objects

to the stacks of garish plastic bowls, shopping baskets, garlands

of glossy chilies and piles of cheap lurid blankets in the markets.

MEXICO

Right To imitate, let alone re-create, a sense of Mexico, I felt it essential to try
to grasp the Mexicans' complete sense of abandonment to the joy of big bold
colour. Here the living room becomes a landscape for the elements within it.
A basketweave bull's head hung on the wall, a broom for sweeping away the
all-pervading desert sand, logs for the fire and painted oil drums used as
containers for cacti, bring a sense of the outdoors indoors. To me they suggest
cattle, horses and cowboys – Billy the Kid heading over the border for one last
session in the cantina. It's style with a sense of humour.

thailand

WALKING THROUGH an orchid farm in Thailand is an incredible experience. Canopies of jewel-like flowers stretch as far as the eye can see. Sub-tropical orchids grow naturally by attaching themselves to the uppermost branches of a tree where they can absorb the sunlight and moisture. To cultivate them they must be grown in the same way. Orchid farms use constructions like wooden pagodas with struts and beams to mimic forest trees. The orchids' fleshy tendril-like roots are exposed to the atmosphere and need to be sprayed daily.

Despite their exotic appearance and origin, orchids are not particularly expensive cut flowers in the West – although you do still tend to pay a premium for orchid plants. Dendrobium is the most commonly exported species fromThailand. The flowers arrive at market wrapped in cellophane with their stems inserted into water vials. Tightly packed into shallow cardboard boxes, they look almost squashed flat. When you open the box they literally spring back to life. Anyone who has passed through Bangkok airport will know that you can buy orchids there to take home packaged in exactly the same way. Orchids are much more robust than you would imagine, surviving the long-haul journey to give us weeks of flower-life at home.

The flower colours remind me of the silks that Thailand is famous for – sheer, vibrant, exotic bolts of colour piled high on market stalls or in shop windows, which, in a few hours, can be transformed into shirts, skirts and dresses to your favourite design. The temples, too, are a source of colour inspiration for me, decorated with garlands of flowers.

I remember during one trip to Thailand that in my hotel room there was a bowl of fruit. There wasn't a single fruit I recognized, but I was determined to try them all, even though I didn't know whether I would like any. And I didn't know immediately – it was as though I had to let the flavours develop in my mouth before I could decide. In a similar way there's something about orchids that leads us to accept colours that we wouldn't normally consider having in the home. Rather as you might pick up a T-shirt on a market stall and fall in love with its colour, even though you know it doesn't suit you, colours that you might find over the top in other flowers seem perfectly acceptable in the petals of an orchid. So go ahead and create something gorgeous with orchids, and don't even try to be subtle.

Surprisingly, orchids as cut flowers are not particularly expensive or difficult to find in the West these days, in spite of their exotic appearance and origin.

Left *Orchid flowers tend to begin fairly low down the stem, which can make choosing a vase for them difficult. So, here, I've floated two individual flower heads of 'Vanda' orchids in a shallow bowl of water. I find the detail and beauty of these flowers so powerful and the vivid purple pattern of the petals so mesmerizing that there's no need to use more than two. The colour and texture of the table surface and bowl add an understated elegance.*
Previous pages *A hot-pink pillow tufted with strands of yellow silk thread is surely inspired by the incredible centre of the lotus flower.*

Right *Massed against a backdrop of sheer orange silk, the colours of these dendrobium orchids literally jump off the page. Dendrobiums are currently available in shades of shocking pink, magenta, purple, cream, red and green, sometimes striped. Orchids sold in bunches en masse often have relatively short stems that can look off balance perched at the top of a tall vase. To counteract this effect I've filled the base of this glass cylinder with gem-like beads of coloured glass. Not only do they echo the colour of the flowers, but they also help to hold the stems in place, as well as disguising their length.*

There can be something a little unreal and artificial about orchid

flowers, as if they have been modelled out of wax or tweaked

from scraps of silk. Their petals come in a surprising intensity

of colour, so powerful that you feel you can almost taste it.

Left Cymbidium orchids are sold as single stems, approximately 45cm (18in) in length, each holding between six to 12 flowers. The large fleshy blooms are supported on leaf-like bracts 4cm (1½in) apart. Sometimes you see single flower heads for sale in cellophane boxes, especially around Mother's Day. Here I've used a single cymbidium flower as a corsage by simply pinning it to a shirt with a dressmaker's pin. The vivid yellow petals contrast with the ruby-red markings in the flower's throat and with the jade-green and jet fabric.

ORCHID STEAMERS

It's fun to link flowers for the table to your menu, but not if it means you have to go to extraordinary lengths with colour coordination and attention to detail. Here the connection is obvious without being over-contrived. Bamboo steamers have been filled with vibrant heads of dendrobium orchids. I cut the flowers from the main stem and literally piled them into the steamer. They are thick and fleshy and will last out of water for the duration of dinner. If you want the display to last longer, though, you can achieve the same effect with the help of florist's foam.

1 Cut the main stem of the orchid into 2.5cm (1in) sections, rather than stripping off the flowers individually.

2 Push the base of each section of stem into a block of pre-soaked florist's foam. Make sure that you completely cover the foam with flowers.

Flower Directory

a

Throughout this book I've used all sorts of flowers, foliage and plants to create impressions of countries all over the world, from England to Japan and back. Here you'll find them gathered together in alphabetical order, with page references to indicate which section they appear in. Use these pages as a quick guide to discover when a flower is in season or the colours it comes in or for brief notes on how it can be used.

Turn to the final page of the directory for some general tips on flower care, from cutting stems to keeping the water clear.

Air plant
(Tillandsia)
Page 133
Plant
Colours: grey-green, pink, red
Availability: all year
This is the ultimate low-maintenance houseplant – it needs no soil to survive, just water. Its shape and colour make it ideal for modern minimalist designs.

Allium
(Allium)
Page 50, 74, 77
Cut flower
Colours: purple, white
Availability: summer
Flowers range from large airy globes to small colourful cones. Alliums are related to onions and you need to change the water frequently to stop an oniony smell developing.

Amaranthus
(Amaranthus)
Page 124, 126
Cut flower
Colours: red, green
Availability: summer
The soft tasselled flowers have the texture of crushed velvet.

Amaryllis
(Hippeastrum)
Pages 90, 112
Cut flower, plant
Colours: white, green, peach, pink, burgundy
Availability: autumn, winter, spring
Big modern-looking flowers on tall straight stems, which are particularly good for contemporary designs.

Anthurium
(Anthurium)
Pages 23, 24, 30
Cut flower, plant
Colours: peach, pink, white, red, burgundy, green, brown
Availability: all year
Use these long-lasting artificial-looking flowers for tropical designs or in ultra-modern interiors.

Arum lily, Calla lily
(Zantedeschia)
Pages 14, 82, 116
Cut flower, plant
Colours: white, yellow, orange, purple, pink, green
Availability: all year
Their clean lines and graphic flowers make these lilies good for contemporary designs.

Aspidistra
(Aspidistra elatior)
Pages 104, 105
Cut foliage, plant
Colours: green or variegated leaves
Availability: all year
The leaves are ideal for disguising containers or blocks of florist's foam since they are flexible enough to wrap around objects and can be fastened with double-sided tape.

Astilbe
(Astilbe)
Page 47
Cut flower, plant
Colours: white, pink, lilac
Availability: summer to early autumn
These light feathery flowers have a country feel that is enhanced by their pastel colours.

b

BANANA
(Musa)
Page 26
Cut flower
Colours: purple, pink
Availability: all year
Still very much a newcomer to the cut-flower market and, as such, a bit of an investment, but worth it for its eye-catching dramatic impact.

BANKSIA
(Banksia)
Page 80
Cut flower
Colours: brown, orange
Availability: summer, autumn, winter
These tough plants hardly look like flowers in the conventional sense, but they are just right for tropical designs or bold modern interiors.

BIRD-OF-PARADISE FLOWER
(Strelitzia)
Page 78
Cut flower
Colours: orange, blue
Availability: all year
Architectural flowers that are long lasting and amazingly contemporary. Even a single stem can have a big impact in the right setting.

BLUEBELL (commercially grown)
(Scilla)
Page 50
Cut flower, plant
Colours: blue, white
Availability: spring
A quintessentially country flower, even though the commercially grown bluebell is not the same species as the woodland plant. The flowers are delicately scented.

c

CALLA LILY, SEE ARUM LILY

CAMELLIA
(Camellia)
Pages 104, 105, 107
Cut flower, plant
Colours: pink, white, red, cream, purple, bicoloured
Availability: spring
Camellia flowers are rather like roses. They lend themselves to anything, from country arrangements to dramatic oriental displays.

CARNATION
(Dianthus)
Pages 19, 65, 66
Cut flower
Colours: white, cream, pink, green, red, purple, burgundy, brown
Availability: all year
The flowers work well in both traditional or modern designs, and come in a surprising range of colours. White blooms have the strongest scent.

CELOSIA
(Celosia)
Page 126
Cut flower
Colours: red, orange, purple, green
Availability: spring, summer, autumn
This is a flower with real texture to it, velvety and downy.

CHRYSANTHEMUM
(Dendranthema)
Page 106
Cut flower, plant
Colours: white, green, pink, lilac, purple, brown, cream, peach
Availability: all year
There are a vast number of shapes, sizes, varieties and colours of chrysanthemum to choose from. The green varieties have an unmistakable oriental look to them.

CORNFLOWER
(Centaurea)
Page 52
Cut flower
Colours: white, lilac, blue
Availability: late spring, early summer
The perfect flower for simple country designs, especially if you want an arrangement to look as though it's come straight from the garden.

CROWN IMPERIAL
(Fritillaria imperialis)
Page 88
Cut flower
Colours: yellow, orange
Availability: spring
The tall lily-like flowers are typical country flowers but they can be used in more formal designs, too.

CYMBIDIUM ORCHID
(Cymbidium)
Pages 115, 148
Cut flower, plant
Colours: white, green, yellow, pink, purple
Availability: all year
Intricately shaped and coloured flowers that last well and can be as show-stopping as a piece of jewellery.

d   e   f

Dahlia
(Dahlia)
Page 76
Cut flower, plant
Colours: white, yellow, orange, red, purple
Availability: spring, summer, autumn
From shaggy-petalled blooms to flower heads as tight as a pompom, dahlias can appear ultra-modern or very traditional – it all depends on the setting and the way you choose to display them.

Dendrobium orchid
(Dendrobium)
Pages 114, 146, 150
Cut flower, plant
Colours: white, green, yellow, pink, purple
Availability: all year
For a flower that's so exotic and grown so far away, these orchids are relatively inexpensive and can be used in many different ways. Mass them in bunches of dazzling colour or pile the loose heads in bowls or baskets – they'll last an evening out of water.

Echeveria
(Echeveria)
Pages 73, 135
Plant
Colour: burgundy and grey foliage
Availability: all year
Succulents such as echeveria immediately evoke a hot arid climate. Individual rosettes of leaves can be used to add a textural element to modern arrangements. Create fake stems for single rosettes either by using cocktail sticks or strong florist's wire – this will help you to position them more precisely.

Forsythia
(Forsythia)
Page 108, 109
Cut flower
Colour: yellow
Availability: spring
Commercially grown stems of forsythia are tall and straight. Use them en masse for a bold minimalist effect. When cutting forsythia from the garden straight stems are a lot harder to find. Use these irregular branches for less formal designs, whether oriental or country style.

g

GARDENIA
(Gardenia)
Pages 55, 58, 59
Cut flower, plant
Colour: white
Availability: winter
One of the most luxurious flowers there is, with a heavenly delicate scent. Gardenias are real hothouse flowers – blooms to be treasured.

GENISTA
(Genista)
Pages 20, 21
Cut flower
Colours: white, pink, peach, yellow
Availability: spring
Delicate scented small flowers on naturally arching stems, ideal for creating a graceful dome-shaped arrangement.

GERANIUM
(Pelargonium)
Pages 19, 136, 137
Cut flower, plant
Colours: white, pink, red, peach, burgundy, lilac
Availability: spring, summer
For many people geraniums aren't an obvious choice as a cut flower, but their delicate flower heads come in some interesting variations – shaped like rose buds or apple blossom. Look out for varieties with scented foliage.

GLADIOLUS
(Gladiolus)
Page 13
Cut flower
Colours: white, red, burgundy, pink, green, yellow, peach
Availability: winter, spring
The way to make the most of gladioli is to mass the stems together for a modern look – anything else just looks too dull and traditional.

GLORY LILY
(Gloriosa superba)
Page 68
Cut flower, plant
Colours: red and yellow bicoloured
Availability: all year
An exotic climbing plant with striped flowers that lend an instant oriental flavour to a design.

GRAPE HYACINTH
(Muscari)
Page 52
Cut flower, plant
Colours: blue, blue and white
Availability: winter, spring
These delicately scented flowers are strongly associated with spring and are ideal for use in country arrangements.

GREVILLEA
(Grevillea)
Page 80
Cut flower
Colour: yellow
Availability: all year
A tough species that is far from conventionally flower-like but has huge potential in modern interiors or a masculine work environment. Get your money's worth by letting the flowers dry for semi-permanent designs.

h

HELICONIA
(Heliconia)
Page 33
Cut flower
Colours: pink, yellow, white, brown
Availability: all year
Occasionally referred to as ginger lilies, these bold tropical flowers are modern and sculptural.

HELLEBORE
(Helleborus)
Page 46
Cut flower, plant
Colours: green, purple, white
Availability: winter, spring
Pretty country flowers that can hold their own even if arranged singly in narrow vases.

HYACINTH
(Hyacinthus)
Page 91
Cut flower, plant, dormant bulb
Colours: white, peach, pink, lilac, cream, blue
Availability: winter to late spring
Hyacinths have a wonderful fragrance. Individual flowers stripped from the stem are ideal for incorporating into bridal bouquets. When working with growing hyacinth bulbs you can also make a positive feature of the bulbs' attractive papery skin.

HYDRANGEA
(Hydrangea macrophylla)
Pages 42, 47, 50, 51, 52, 53, 81
Cut flower, plant
Colours: white, pink, lilac, blue, burgundy, green
Availability: spring, summer, autumn, early winter
Long-stemmed flowers give a big bold modern look. They can also be dried for wreaths and garlands. Leave them to dry gradually in water so that they keep their shape and firm stem.

j

l

m

JASMINE
(Jasminum officinale)
Page 19
Cut flower, plant
Colours: white, white-pink
Availability: late spring, early summer
The small flowers have a strong fragrance, and the trailing stems make them ideal for bridal bouquets. If you can't buy the cut flowers, buy a pot plant instead and cut the trailing stems from this. Some plants come trained on frames so you may need to disentangle them carefully. Jasmine can be planted directly into the garden where it will grow into a substantial creeper.

LILAC
(Syringa)
Page 45, 50
Cut flower
Colours: white, lilac
Availability: winter, spring
Unfortunately, commercially grown lilac has no perfume but it does tend to be longer lasting than the home-grown variety and is particularly good for country arrangements.

LILY
(Lilium)
Page 42
Cut flower, plant
Colours: white, cream, green, pink, red, yellow, burgundy, orange
Availability: all year
These flowers come in an endless assortment of colours and forms, many with heavy perfumes.

LILY OF THE VALLEY
(Convallaria majalis)
Pages 59, 60
Cut flower, plant
Colour: white
Availability: winter
Sweetly scented, romantic flowers that are popular for bridal bouquets or for simple massed posies.

LOTUS
(Nelumbo)
Pages 128, 143
Cut flower
Colours: white, purple, pink, yellow
Availability: late winter, spring
This tropical flower is a close relative of the water lily, which may be slightly easier to buy as a cut flower. Also available as dried seed pods.

MAGNOLIA
(Magnolia)
Pages 112, 119
Cut foliage
Colours: leaves green above, brown below
Availability: all year
This strong long-lasting foliage with a brown suede-like underside is invaluable for wreaths and any other designs where contrasting textures are needed.

MARGUERITE
(Argyranthemum)
Page 48
Cut flower, plant
Colours: white and yellow
Availability: spring, early summer
Marguerites are pretty daisy-type flowers that are particularly suited to country designs.

MARIGOLD
(Calendula)
Page 122
Cut flower, plant
Colours: yellow, orange
Availability: all year
Traditional country flowers that can also be used in more imaginative ways to capitalize on their explosive colour and massed petals.

n

o

p

Narcissus
(Narcissus)
Page 88
Cut flower, plant
Colours: white, cream, orange, yellow
Availability: winter, spring
For maximum impact, mass the small exquisitely scented flower heads together. Varying the stem length or the angle at which you bind them can create shapely domes of flowers. Cutting the stems causes them to 'bleed' a sticky sap but flower foods specifically designed for narcissi will minimize the effect. Growers have managed to extend their season slightly but narcissi are still true spring flowers.

Olive
(Olea)
Page 18
Cut foliage, plant
Colour: silver-grey foliage
Availability: all year
Suddenly the olive is the shrub of the moment and growers are constantly presenting us with new variations. Some bushes have coiled spring-like stems or stems that have been plaited together when young and flexible. Use the long-lasting foliage for wreaths or incorporate pot plants into semi-permanent displays. Olive trees are the chic new alternatives to the topiary bay trees that so predictably grace the front door at smart addresses.

Pansy
(Viola x wittrockiana)
Page 43
Cut flower, plant
Colours: bicoloured black, white, pink, lilac, blue, orange
Availability: spring, early summer
These are charming naïve flowers for country arrangements that are still somewhat rare as a cut flower but easy to buy as a pot plant.

Peony
(Paeonia)
Pages 42, 45, 47, 50
Cut flower
Colours: pink, white, peach, red, cerise
Availability: late spring, early summer
Romantic voluptuous flowers that come either packed with petals or with a central crown of contrasting stamens.

Phalaenopsis orchid
(Phalaenopsis)
Page 111
Cut flower, plant
Colour: white
Availability: all year
The graceful stems of this orchid say sheer elegance and luxury.

Philodendron
(Philodendron)
Page 28
Cut foliage, plant
Colours: green or variegated leaves
Availability: all year
The leaves of the philodendron, often called elephant's ears for obvious reasons, are so vast and dramatic that just one in a vase can make a big impact in a modern interior.

r

s

Poppy

(Papaver)
Pages 20, 21
Cut flower
Colours: white, cream, peach, pink, yellow, orange
Availability: spring, summer, autumn
Gorgeous papery pleated petals that can be used in modern designs as well as in more country-inspired arrangements. The dried seed heads are also available.

Protea

(Protea)
Pages 38, 39, 40
Cut flower
Colours: pink, white, orange
Availability: summer, autumn, winter
Bold masculine flowers that last well in water but also dry easily. Ideal for tropical or bold modern designs.

Ranunculus

(Ranunculus)
Pages 10, 16
Cut flower, plant
Colours: white, pink, peach, yellow, red, orange
Availability: autumn, winter, spring
Rustic country flowers like colourful buttercups, to which they're closely related. Bunches of mixed colours look good in earthenware. Buy them in tight bud if possible and they should last about two weeks.

Rose

(Rosa)
Pages 42, 51, 57, 59, 61, 63, 92, 93, 94, 96, 98, 99, 110, 114, 118, 121, 124, 125
Cut flower
Colours: white, pink, lilac, peach, red, green, orange, brown
Availability: all year
Roses on long stems spell glamour; those with full open flowers say country garden. Twist the petals from the flower heads to use them in lots of different ways or build the heads into shapes using florist's foam.

Snake grass

(Equisetum hyemalis)
Page 104
Cut flower
Colour: green
Availability: all year
This grass has strong bamboo like stems that can be cut into lengths and bound into bundles to add structure and form to oriental designs.

Snakeshead fritillary

(Fritillaria meleagris)
Page 46
Cut flower, plant
Colours: purple, green
Availability: spring
Pretty country flowers for simple spring designs – this is a species that hasn't yet been persuaded to grow outside its natural season.

Stephanotis

(Stephanotis)
Page 59
Cut flower, plant
Colour: white
Availability: all year
The flowers have a truly heady fragrance. Individual flower heads can be stripped from the stems and are ideal for bridal bouquets.

Strelitzia, see Bird-of-paradise flower

Sweet pea

(Lathyrus odoratus)
Pages 45, 50
Cut flower
Colours: pink, white, peach, red, lilac, purple
Availability: late spring, early summer
Scented, old-fashioned cottage garden flowers for country arrangements.

t

Tuberose

(Polianthes tuberosa)
Pages 13, 15
Cut flower
Colour: creamy pink
Availability: all year
Beautifully scented flowers. The individual flower heads can be stripped from the stem and are ideal for bridal bouquets.

Tulip

(Tulipa)
Pages 13, 85, 86
Cut flower
Colours: white, pink, yellow, cream, orange, purple, red
Availability: all year
Tulips are available all year round now, not just in spring, but those on sale in summer tend not to be so robust as flowers grown in their natural season. Although they are a country flower, you can achieve some surprisingly modern designs with them.

v

Vanda orchid

(Vanda)
Page 144
Cut flower
Colours: purple and white
Availability: all year
The sheer intensity of colour and the intricacy of pattern is best appreciated on the individual flower heads – by floating them on water, for example. Vanda orchid flowers can last several weeks on the stem. Keep them cool air and mist with water from time to time.The flowers are sensitive to ethylene gas which is produced by ripening fruit and vegetables and by the dying flowers, so snip off old flower heads as soon as they fade.

HOW TO GET THE MOST FROM YOUR CUT FLOWERS

The stems of most cut flowers start to dry out as soon as they are out of water for any length of time. Before you start to arrange flowers, recut their stems using florist's scissors: take off 2cm (just under an inch) to expose fresh fibres. Cutting the stems at an angle increases the surface area exposed to the water and maximizes uptake.

If flowers are going to be pushed into florist's foam, cut them at the sharpest angle possible so that end end is almost needle-like.

Any leaves on the stem that will be underwater in an arrangement should be stripped off, or they will rot and turn the water slimy.

Change the water in a vase every day and the flowers will last longer. There's no need to redo the arrangement – just stand the vase in the sink under a running tap until the water is replenished.

Always use flower food when it is supplied with cut flowers. It's not a gimmick – it really does prolong their life and keep the water clear.

ACKNOWLEDGMENTS

I've learned that you begin each book with a wonderful sense of excitement and a terrible fear of failure. I approach each day of photography in a dreadful state of nerves and lacking confidence, worrying whether I can deliver what I so desperately want to achieve. I've also learned that a book's success isn't totally dependent on me: it is about assembling a team where each person makes their own extremely valuable contribution. On this book the team has been fantastic and I would like to sincerely thank them all.

Tom, for his fantastic photography and his consistent patience and calmness.

Lyndsay, for her energy, enthusiasm, amazing eye and attention to detail, and for coming to the rescue in our moment of need.

Magnus, for his fabulousness, gossip and, of course, hard work.

Chi, for believing in us and calmly steering the book in the right direction – it couldn't have happened without you.

Sam, for his understanding of our vision with his fantastic layouts.

Sharon and Helen, for their patience and help with the text.

Zia, for her endless help, patience and more patience.

My staff at Jane Packer, for consistently backing me up when I called for urgent reinforcements, and for their help, hard work and dedication in making our company what it is. Thank you.

Metz Van Kleef of Holland, for generous help with supplying top-quality flowers and information.

The Atlantic Bar & Grill, for generously allowing us to photograph within their unique surroundings.

Best of New Covent Garden Market, for help and assistance with containers and accessories.

Chanel and Dior, for the kind loan of the vintage perfume bottles.

And, of course, my family who help and support me constantly. Gary, Rebby and Lola, you make it all worthwhile – what would I be with out you?